D1567183

# English in Action

By Wally Cirafesi

**Learn How to Teach English Using the Bible**

Illustrations by Toni Summers

Teacher's Manual

*English in Action: Learn How to Teach English Using the Bible (Teacher's Manual)* by Wally Cirafesi

© 2006 by Wally Cirafesi. All rights reserved. This material may not be repro-
duced in any form without written permission from the author. Photocopy permission, for in-class use only, is given for the handouts.

Illustrations by Toni Summers.
Illustrations © 1995, 1998 by Toni Summers. All rights reserved. Permission is
granted to reproduce the illustrations for classroom use only.

Published by
**dawson**media

a ministry of The Navigators
P.O. Box 6000, Colorado Springs, CO 80934
www.dawsonmedia.com

First edition 1994. Fifth edition 2006.

All Scriptures quoted from The Holy Bible, New Century Version,
© 1987, 1988, 1991 by Word Publishing, Dallas, Texas 75039.
Used by permission.

ISBN 0-9638273-0-8

Printed in the United States of America.

# Contents

## SECTION B: TEACHER'S GUIDE FOR THE STUDENT WORKBOOK

## SECTION C: ENGLISH-OUTREACH MINISTRY

# About the Author

Wally Cirafesi has been with The Navigators since 1975. He received his B.S. degree in English Education from Penn State University and his master's degree in TESOL from Ohio State University. He and his wife, Connie, learned Spanish, using TPR principles, while living in Venezuela for nine years. Wally has led numerous training sessions in ESL for laypeople and currently directs the TESOL program at Moody Bible Institute.

# Dedication

To Connie, my best friend, loving wife and faithful companion in the life of faith to which God has called us.

# Acknowledgments

I am indebted, first of all, to Dr. James Asher of San Jose State University, the creator of the Total Physical Response (TPR) method. His book, *Learning Another Language Through Actions: The Complete Teacher's Guide,* gives the origins of TPR's development and answers some 175 frequently asked questions about TPR. Pointers in explaining TPR techniques were drawn from Ramiro Garcia's book, *Instructor's Notebook: How To Apply TPR For Best Results.** Both books would be a great help to you for additional input on TPR.

Many of the ideas on the Expansion Activities pages and the procedure for teaching a Sequence were gained from my experience in using Maxine Frauman-Prickel and Noriko Takahashi's book, *Action English Pictures,* and Elizabeth Romijn and Contee Seely's book, *Live Action English.*

I would like to thank Mr. Waldron Scott for his enthusiastic support of the ESL program in Paterson, New Jersey. A warm thank-you goes to Diana Umpierre, Bruce Marcum, Steve Stookesberry and especially Ken Johns and Second Presbyterian Church in Memphis, Tennessee, for their financial gifts. I also want to thank Dr. Betty Sue Brewster, Donna Ladner, Carol Johnson, Howard Pollock, the Reverend Ezequiel Romero and Kathy Woods for their insights on improving the books. A big thank-you goes to the volunteer teachers who field-tested the books and also gave valuable feedback: Mary Jo Plemmons, Jone Reid, Kathy Compton, Elena Romero, John Pickering, Neiva Garcia, Brenda Mainer, Rebecca Garcia and Rachel Romero. Thanks also to Toni Summers for her work on the illustrations, Mike Hames on layout and Tina Clark on editing. A special thanks to my friend Larry Blake for his listening ear, constant encouragement and personal involvement in making the books become realities.

Most of all, I would like to acknowledge the late Dr. Tom Brewster and his wife, Dr. Betty Sue Brewster, for guiding me through my own learning of Spanish. Many of my convictions about language learning were gained from their tutelage at the Toronto Institute of Linguistics and their "Learning Cycle" program in Cali, Colombia, in 1979.

---

*The Asher and Garcia books may be ordered from Sky Oaks Productions, Inc., P.O. Box 1102, Los Gatos, CA 95031, www.tpr-world.com

# Preface

This Teacher's Manual is an effort to equip LAYPEOPLE to successfully lead Christian outreach ESL (English as a Second Language) groups. It contains all that one needs to begin a Bible-based English program with the companion Student Workbook, *English in Action*. The *English in Action* Teacher's Manual is designed to meet a wide variety of interests, from those who want to have informal English classes with their neighbors to those who desire to begin English outreach programs through churches and agencies.

The Teacher's Manual and Student Workbook have grown out of my experiences in the Navigator ministry, learning Spanish overseas, teaching ESL to adults and conducting numerous lay teacher–training seminars.

I have been privileged to see hundreds of ordinary laypeople successfully lead ESL groups. YOU can do it too! You do not need to be a gifted teacher nor be able to explain fine points of English grammar. If you can speak English, this book will equip you to teach it!

The methodology you will learn is called Total Physical Response (TPR). Students and teachers alike enjoy TPR. The feedback we receive is always enthusiastic. TPR is action-oriented. You will be more like a director of a play than an explainer of the language. Students will enjoy your class, learn lots of English and be personally involved in the Scriptures in the process!

It is my desire that after studying this Manual you will enthusiastically become involved in communicating the Gospel through the teaching of English. The need and demand for English is much too great to be met by professional teachers alone. You, as an English-speaking Christian, have two wonderful gifts to offer peoples of another culture: your language and the Gospel. I sincerely hope this book helps you to use both.

Wally Cirafesi

# Questions You May Have

1. **DO I NEED TO SPEAK THE LANGUAGE OF THE STUDENTS?** No! ESL classes often have a variety of languages represented in the classroom. Not being able to speak the language of your students can be a plus factor for you and for them. It will obligate them to attempt to speak in English more frequently.

2. **DO I NEED TO EXPLAIN ENGLISH GRAMMAR?** No, again! As this Teacher's Manual makes abundantly clear, your role will be to direct the action, not to explain the language.

3. **CAN THE CURRICULUM BE USED WITH ANY LANGUAGE GROUP?** Yes. Any student who has a first-grade literacy level in his or her native language can use *English in Action* beneficially.

4. **WHAT IS THE APPROPRIATE AGE LEVEL FOR *ENGLISH IN ACTION?*** *English in Action* has been successfully field-tested with students ranging in age from 12 to 70.

5. **HOW MANY HOURS IS THE *ENGLISH IN ACTION* CURRICULUM?** It is approximately 76 hours long but can be shortened or lengthened, depending on the teacher's preferences and the students' needs. The Teacher's Manual provides flexibility. There are many optional items and activities that can be used or passed over at the teacher's discretion.

6. **WHAT IS THE TOTAL PHYSICAL RESPONSE (TPR) METHOD?** TPR is a language-acquisition method that emphasizes listening, body movement and the giving of commands. "When the body moves, the brain remembers" is one of the themes of TPR. TPR is a proven method that is truly fun for teachers and students alike.

7. **DOES *ENGLISH IN ACTION* EMPLOY ONLY TPR?** No. A wide variety of methods, activities and exercises is included in the curriculum. TPR is used to lay a foundation of internalized vocabulary from which students expand their abilities.

8. **CAN THE LESSONS BE ADAPTIED TO MORE ADVANCED STUDENTS?** Yes. A full explanation of how to do so is given on page 172.

# An Overview of the Curriculum

Before you begin learning TPR, it is helpful to see where it fits within the overall *English in Action* curriculum. There are four basic components that should be used to get the most out of this Bible-based program.

```
          /\
         /  \ D
        / Expansion \
       / Activities  \ C
      /----------------\
     /  Workbook        \
    /   Exercises        \ B
   /----------------------\
  /   Sequences            \ A
 /--------------------------\
/         TPR                \
------------------------------
```

## A. DO TPR TO TEACH BASIC VOCABULARY.

The first part of the Teacher's Manual will equip you to use TPR in teaching vocabulary. Knowing how to "TPR" basic vocabulary lays the foundation for work with the language. The Beginning Lessons (Chapter 6) serve to help you and the students become comfortable with TPR and provide an essential base of vocabulary, before beginning the Bible Sequences (Chapter 7). TPR serves to **introduce** vocabulary as well as **review** vocabulary throughout the curriculum. You will review the Student Workbook lessons by "TPRing" the vocabulary, not by reciting the Bible Sequences word for word. The TPR approach is based on research about how children learn language. Children hear and use the language for many years before they understand its grammar. TPR follows that pattern. However, adults are not children. They can and often want to speak the language they are learning as quickly as possible. The other components of the curriculum will help in this regard.

## B. DO THE BIBLE SEQUENCES IN THE STUDENT WORKBOOK.

Students will be involved in action stories. Here they go beyond commands to dealing with people in a story context. They learn to tell the stories, as well as write and read them.

## C. DO THE EXERCISES CONTAINED IN EACH CHAPTER OF THE STUDENT WORKBOOK.

After you have prepared the students with TPR and have worked through the Bible Sequences step by step, you can then build on what they have learned by doing the word order, fill-in-the-blank, sentence formation and reading exercises.

## D. DO EXPANSION ACTIVITIES.

After you have done the above three steps, you can expand the students' abilities in listening, speaking, reading or writing by having them participate in a wide variety of communicative activities.

# Teacher Training

Section

# The Total Physical Response Method (TPR)

# Chapter 1

# Introduction to TPR and Language Learning
## Observing a TPR Classroom

This is your first opportunity to observe a TPR classroom. It is the first day of class at the English-language program for Hispanic adults in Paterson, New Jersey. All the students are Beginners (see "Placement Test" in Chapter 3 for skill-level explanations).

You take a seat on the couch in the back. The room has a cozy feel to it. It is carpeted and there is the smell of fresh coffee in the air. About 15 students are seated on folding chairs around two oblong tables.

The teacher begins by explaining in Spanish* the method the students will use to learn English. She says, "You will be learning English similar to the way you learned Spanish. You will listen and then do as I do. You will not be asked to speak until you are ready. I will give a command. First, I will do the action by myself **[Modeling].** Then you will do the action with me **[Together].** Later you will do the action on your own **[Alone].** Finally, in the coming weeks, you will be able to give commands to others **[Role Reversal].**†"

She continues: "Please relax and enjoy our time together. I want you to have fun and not to worry about making mistakes. Everyone makes many mistakes when he or she learns a language. It is unavoidable. You will learn from your mistakes. I will be here to help you step by step. To begin, I need three volunteers to sit in these chairs."

Four chairs, including one for the teacher, are in the front of the room, lined up facing the other students. The teacher tells the other students to listen and watch.

In English, the teacher says, "Stand up." As she says it, only she stands up. Then she says, "Sit down," and she sits down **[Model].** Next she looks at the volunteers and says, "Stand up." As she says it, she stands up and signals for the volunteers to stand up with her. She says, "Sit down," and they all sit. The teacher and the students perform these commands several times together **[Together].** The students do not speak.

---

* If you cannot speak their language, have someone help you, or simply begin.

† Words in **[bold]** with brackets are the names of TPR techniques.

Next the teacher says, "Stand up, sit down," but she hesitates before performing **[Hesitate]**. She looks at the students to see if they have begun to perform. They have, so she performs the action with them to reinforce what they are doing. The teacher says, "Stand up. Walk." She walks and they follow. "Stop." Everyone stops. "Walk." The teacher hesitates. They all walk. "Stop." All stop. "Turn around." The teacher turns around and the students follow. "Walk. Stop. Turn around. Sit down." They all perform together several times **[Together]**.

The teacher now remains seated and gives these commands again, to the volunteers up front, changing their order and pace **[Jumble]**. "Walk. Stop. Stop." (Students laugh.) "Walk. Stop. Turn around. Walk. Stop. Turn around. Sit down." The students respond perfectly **[Alone]**. The teacher and the students applaud their performance.

The teacher now gestures to one of the volunteers to perform her commands. She gives the volunteer a series of commands, pausing after each one: "Stand up. Walk. Stop. Turn around." On hearing "turn around," the student hesitates, unsure of himself. The teacher stands next to him. She says, "Turn around," and she turns around, **Modeling** the action. The student follows the teacher's example. Then she says, pausing after each command, "Walk. Stop. Walk. Stop. Turn around. Walk. Stop." The student performs successfully.

Now the teacher turns her attention to the rest of the class. She calls on three other students and gives them commands, pausing after each one. "Stand up. Walk. Stop. Turn around. Walk. Stop. Turn around. Walk. Stop. Turn around. Sit down" **[Alone]**. The students perform correctly. She calls on other students and gives the same commands but in a different order **[Jumble]**. "Stand up. Sit down. Stand up. Walk. Stop. Turn around. Sit down." More applause. The teacher continues to work with these five commands (stand up, sit down, walk, stop, turn around) until all the students are succeeding. If anyone fails, she immediately **Models** the command.

The teacher is now satisfied that the class can respond to these five commands successfully. She introduces some new ones. "Point to the table." She points to the table **[Model]**. Students listen. "Point to the table." Students follow her lead **[Together]**. She calls on the volunteers. "Stand up. Walk. Stop. Turn around. Point to the table." The students do the action with her. She tells one volunteer, "Stand up. Point to the table. Sit down." The student performs perfectly. The teacher applauds. She gives a series of commands to several other students. A few of them hesitate. She models the action for them. They then follow her lead. The students are obviously having fun. They are relaxed. The teacher is patient with them. She is quick to model for anyone who is unsure of a given command.

Next, she gives a command and performs by herself. "Stand up. Walk to the table. Point to the table. Touch the table." ("Touch" is new.) She continues. "Touch the table. Touch the book. Touch the pencil." She continues to **Model** and do commands together using "touch." She gives them a series of commands. This time she gestures to the students to listen to three commands before they perform. "Stand up. Point to the table. Touch the table" **[Chain Commands].** Next she says, "Turn around. Point to the book. Sit down." She varies the order of the commands, but the students perform without trouble. She calls on others and gives some new combinations, pausing after each one. "Stand up. Walk to the table. Touch the pencil" **[Novelty].** "Point to the book. Touch the table. Point to the table."

She continues working with "touch," "point to," "table," "book" and "pencil" until students are successful. If they fail, she **Models** for them. She then begins to combine commands. "Stand up and walk to the table." "Touch the table and sit down" **[Connectives].** Students perform well. She continues combining commands until the students are having continual success in responding.

The last 15 minutes of the class, she writes the vocabulary from the lesson on the board. She then writes some commands that were used in class. As she writes them, she acts them out to ensure understanding. Students copy the words into their workbooks.

The class is over. It was obvious that the students had fun. They laughed spontaneously and applauded in a relaxed atmosphere. Only the teacher had spoken. The students listened and performed. Some were eager to perform, while others were shy. The teacher encouraged the shy ones by emphasizing **Modeling** and **Together.** She made certain they succeeded.

## TWO WEEKS LATER:

The teacher is in front of the room holding Beginning Lesson pages from the first two weeks of lessons. She uses the pages to generate commands that review previous material. (To review, she uses **Alone, Jumble, Chain Commands, Connectives** and **Role Reversal.**) She chooses any of these techniques to help with review. There is no particular order in doing so. The review is all action. None of the language used is new. No one writes.

She begins, "Carlos, stand up and turn around twice slowly" **[Connectives].** Carlos performs. "Walk to the table. Pick up the pencil. Put the pencil *in* the bag" **[Chain].** Carlos performs, but puts the pencil *on* the bag. The teacher repeats,

"Put the pencil *in* the bag." Carlos does not understand. The teacher **Models.** She says to Carlos, "Put the pencil *in* the bag." Carlos succeeds. She continues, "Carlos, walk to the table. Pick up the red book and put the book in the box." Carlos hesitates again when he gets to "in the box." The teacher picks up a book and, as she **Models,** she says, "in the box," "on the box." Carlos understands. She says, "Put the ball in the bag." Carlos performs correctly.

The teacher continues for 5 to 10 minutes, working with other students as she did with Carlos.

Then she takes out cue cards displaying the vocabulary the students have practiced for two weeks. She calls on Carmela. She shows Carmela three cards: "walk," "touch" and "pick up." Carmela calls on Olga and says, "Walk to the table. Touch your nose. Pick up the basket" **[Role Reversal].** Olga performs perfectly. The teacher now tells Olga to do the same with Carmela. Olga says, "Walk. Touch the desk. Pick up the pencil." Carmela performs **[Role Reversal].** This continues with other students for another 10 minutes.

The teacher then breaks the class into small groups. Each group has someone who feels confident enough to speak. That student uses cue cards to direct the behavior of others in the group. The teacher is circulating from group to group, helping and encouraging the students to direct behavior and respond to commands. The center of attention is now away from the teacher and on the students.

There is laughter in the small groups and **everyone is involved in using the language.** This goes on for another 10 minutes. The teacher is now confident that most of the class is having success.

She is ready to introduce new material.

The classrooms you have just "observed" have given you a glimpse of TPR. I would like now to help you understand better the "What," "Why" and "How" of what was going on in those classes.

With TPR, it is especially important to **understand how and why it works.** If you do not, you will naturally slip into the teacher role of explaining the language. Explaining the language has its place, but it is a low priority in TPR. Do not be concerned with explaining the language. Think of yourself not as a teacher but rather as a *director* of a play. Your role will be to direct the students in **using the language.**

# What Is TPR?

## A. TPR IS A METHOD OF LANGUAGE LEARNING BASED ON THREE KEY IDEAS:

1) Listening: It has been called "the comprehension approach."

2) Body movement: Students perform what they hear.

3) Commands: Teacher and students direct behavior by giving commands.

# The Value of Listening, Body Movement and Commands

## A. COMPREHENSION-BASED LEARNING

1) Listening! listening! listening! is emphasized in TPR.

   *Why?*

   a) A person cannot produce what he or she cannot hear. For that reason, the ears are the first "target" in TPR. Students listen for days and sometimes weeks before they are expected to speak.

   b) The brain begins to digest the language even before a person can reproduce it. In my early days of learning Spanish, I listened to countless hours of continuous "loop" cassettes. This helped my ears adjust to the sounds of the language.

   c) Confidence will build in overcoming the first barrier to language learning—the tension created by the question, "Will I understand what is said to me?"

2) TPR, however, is not passive listening. Students listen in order to perform, not in order to take notes.

## B. BODY MOVEMENT–BASED LEARNING

**"When the body moves, the brain remembers."**

1) **Long-term memory is activated** when one becomes physically involved in learning. Performing commands for 5 minutes with the verb "throw" will register more deeply in the brain than with 10 minutes of written exercises or the memorizing of a sentence using the verb "throw."

Recently a middle-aged friend was telling me about several things he remembered making in his ninth-grade woodshop class. When I asked him what he did in his ninth-grade English class, he gave me a blank stare!

2) Body movement **connects language with experience.** Students experience the language as they hear it, not only by performing commands but also by being placed in situations that help them to remember the language. If, for example, the first time a student hears the word "scratch" it is in the command, "Scratch your nose with the banana," he or she will likely remember "scratch" because it was learned in a humorous situation.

3) Body movement can be helpful (and fun) when learning word order or other aspects of grammar and not just commands.

For example, I have students make a cue card for each word and punctuation mark that follows: Your/name/ is/ Jose/ ./?/ (six cards). I give one card to each of six students. Facing the class, the group holds the cards and arranges itself into as many correct sentences as possible.

As they rearrange themselves to change a statement into a question or vice-versa, students are physically involved in learning English word order. The retention is better and they have fun doing it.

## C. COMMAND-BASED LEARNING

1) We hear and give commands constantly in daily life. Would you like to count the number of times a day that you either give or receive commands? The **frequency of use** makes commands an excellent place to begin.

2) Studies have revealed that as much as **40% of vocabulary used in the workplace** is the imperative.*

---

* *Live Action English,* by Elizabeth Romijn and Contee Seely.

For example:   "Put that box on the desk."
              "Give me the hammer."

3)   Commands **get people moving,** and that is what we want!

4)   Commands are especially **easy to use** in English.

There are numerous ways in Spanish to give the command "walk," depending to whom you are talking: anda, ande, andemos, anden. In English, the verb remains the same, "walk."

5)   Commands are **the root,** or base, **form** of verbs. We build on them. When students have mastered the command forms of verbs, it is easier to move on to other forms (walk, walking, walked, will walk).

6)   Commands can be used to work on other tenses, not just the present tense.

a)   The past tense:   "Olga, touch the table."
                       "Luly, if Olga touched the table, stand up."

b)   The future tense:   "When I clap, you will stand up."

# Internalizing Is the Goal

**A. INTERNALIZING** the language, not memorizing, is the goal. This is an important distinction.

1)   Memorizing is recalling an exact copy of something, such as a telephone number, when needed. Memorizing often leads to overload. Students' heads become filled with information about the language, which they cannot put into practice. They may know a lot but use very little of what they know.

2)   Internalizing is learning to manipulate the language in a variety of situations. That is why in TPR the focus is on using verbs in countless commands and situations rather than on memorizing vocabulary.

# Proven Results of TPR

**A. TPR LOWERS ANXIETY FOR STUDENTS**. This is important! Anxiety is a major obstacle in language learning. Everyone tends to feel uptight in language class. I strongly disliked my high school French class. The teacher made me so nervous, I would head for cover whenever she started asking questions!

*How does TPR lower anxiety?*

1) **By the use of modeling.** You, the teacher, will **Model** (do first) what you expect the students to do. You also perform actions with them. They soon realize that you are at their side helping them to perform. You are not trying to trick them or put them on the spot.

2) **TPR is fun.** If you relax and have fun with the commands, your students will also. Funny, crazy commands are to be encouraged!

3) **Student success is the goal.** This too is important! As mentioned above, you are not out to trick the students. Your goal is that they successfully respond to commands. If they hesitate, you jump right in to help them. You build daily on their successes.

4) **There is no pressure to speak.** You will not be pressuring them to speak from the first day as some other methods do. You will encourage them to speak when they are ready. Some will need to be "gently pushed," but not pressured, to speak.

**B. TPR LEADS TO RAPID UNDERSTANDING.** You will be amazed at how much students can understand after only a few days of TPR. Growth in comprehension usually is like an airplane taking off; there is an immediate surge upward, but then a leveling off. However, with TPR, even after the initial surge (three to four weeks), comprehension should continue to grow steadily.

**C. TPR LEADS TO RAPID CREATIVE USE OF THE LANGUAGE.** Within a few weeks students begin to create their own commands. With TPR you can constantly encourage creative expression.

**D. HIGH STUDENT INVOLVEMENT** (doing, observing, telling) is a part of

TPR. It is more difficult for boredom to creep into the TPR classroom!

**E. TPR OFTEN CREATES HIGH MOTIVATION IN STUDENTS.** Our experience, and that of others, is that students enjoy TPR. When one course ends, they often cannot wait for the next one to begin. This contrasts with the high drop-out rate of traditional approaches.

# A Word about Goals for a TPR Program

TPR is most profitably used with Beginners and Low Intermediates (see Placement Test in Chapter 3). Whether you are doing basic TPR lessons, such as are found in Chapter 6's "Beginning Lessons," or whether you are working on Chapter 7's "Bible Sequences," keep in mind the following key words as your basic goals: Attitude, Comprehension and Function. If the students are making progress in these areas, you are "on target."

**A. ATTITUDE:** Most students enter language learning fearful and uncertain of their ability to learn a new language. The goal is to CHANGE THAT ATTITUDE. We want each student to experience success, which results in an enthusiastic desire to continue to learn English. Without an attitude change, the majority of students drop out.

**B. COMPREHENSION:** The goal is that each student understand and INTERNALIZE all the vocabulary, most importantly the verbs. Presented to them through TPR, they will be able to successfully perform a variety of commands for each verb in the course.

**C. FUNCTION:** The goal is that each student experiences success in USING survival vocabulary. Success includes understanding, performing and speaking.

# Principles of Language Learning

Understanding some basic principles of language learning will increase your confidence in the classroom and in dealing with student expectations.

### A. LANGUAGE LEARNING IS A SOCIAL ACTIVITY, NOT AN ACADEMIC ONE.

*Why is this important to know?*

1) Because students will expect you to teach them the language. The fact of the matter is that you can't! Languages are learned by using them, not simply by studying them.

2) Thus, your real goal is not to teach them about English, but rather to help them in their attempts to use it.

3) Initially, some students react to TPR as childish, without realizing, I might add, just how insightful that is. It seems the higher the education possessed by the student the stronger "study mentality" they bring to the classroom. But do not fear! Most catch on quickly and realize they are learning. Showing them the Student Workbook will help them to realize that TPR will be part of an integrated program.

4) Since language is LEARNED, not taught nor studied, they must be willing to learn it. Your role is to direct the learning process. Their role is to use what you give them.

### B. LEARN A *LITTLE* AND USE IT A *LOT*.

1) This is a BIGGIE! Unfortunately, this principle is violated in many approaches to language learning. Many methods overload students with information *about* the language. Much more is given than can be used. The

LEARN        USE IT

usual result is frustration!

2) Following this principle—learn a little and use it a lot—enables the learner to: a) focus on using the language;

    b)  retain what he uses;

    c)  avoid overload;

    d)  experience success and gain confidence.

3) As the teacher, YOU may find it difficult to follow this principle. Remind yourself: "Slow and steady wins the race." Concentrate on the success of the students. If they are consistently succeeding, your pace is fine. If they are failing often, you are probably going too fast.

4) The principle is not "learn a little and REPEAT it a lot." A lot of repetition produces anxiety and boredom.

5) If students are able to use ONE item of language today that they were unable to use yesterday, they are making significant progress.

6) Language is explosive. A little becomes a lot quickly, so do not be in a hurry. After only the first lesson, students will be able to respond to dozens of commands.

## C. "CHALKING AND TALKING" HAVE A WAY OF "BALKING" THE LEARNING PROCESS.

1) Resist the temptation to constantly explain the language. Occasional explanations can be helpful and necessary. Regularly stopping to explain items, however, can become a burden to you and boring to the students.

2) When a student is confused, if possible, DEMONSTRATE and INVOLVE the students in trying to clarify or correct.

For example, during Sequence #1 a student may ask, "Does the word 'feel' in line 4 and line 9 mean the same thing?" (4. Feel the apple; 9. You feel sad.) Instead of explaining the meaning of the words, demonstrate the difference in meaning with actions.

## D. EARS BEFORE EYES.

1) The first emphasis in TPR is to "train the ears."

2) In the beginning a learner's ears are "slow." A new language always sounds so fast, but that is not really the case. Our ears simply have to adjust to its sounds.

3) We want to connect their ears to sounds, not to written words, especially in the beginning. They need to develop confidence in their ears. In everyday life, people will **speak** to them, not give them written explanations!

4) A goal is to break the natural cycle students use: from "hear—translate—do" to "hear—do."

I once had a delightful elderly student named Pedro. Pedro, after hearing a command in English, would always whisper the translation to himself in Spanish first. Then he would give himself a reassuring nod and begin to perform. As soon as I saw his lips begin to move I would jokingly take out my pretend scissors and cut the words right out of his mouth!

5) We also want to make certain students can hear and perform vocabulary before they are expected to write. This pattern is followed throughout the *English in Action* curriculum.

## E. SPEAKING SHOULD BE GENTLY ENCOURAGED, NOT FORCED.

1) When? As students demonstrate a readiness to do so. Some will be eager in the first or second week, while others will need to be nudged after a few weeks.

Bernarda was a middle-aged woman who would "freeze" whenever she was called upon. I waited weeks before asking her to give commands. Gradually, I gave her simple commands to repeat. As she experienced success, she began to relax and participate more freely.

2) Adult learners are not babies. They need to, and often want to, speak as soon as possible. You should encourage them to do so.

3)  As they hear more accurately, they will speak more accurately.

4)  TPR should move progressively from teacher-directed to student-directed action. Usually by the second week, some students are speaking. By the fifth or sixth week most, if not all, students should be involved in giving commands.

## F.  PRONUNCIATION IS "FRAGILE — HANDLE WITH CARE"

A student's attempts at pronunciation are like a child's homemade gifts to a parent. The gifts usually do not look good, but they are the best the child can do!* In the same vein, receive your students' pronunciation attempts warmly.

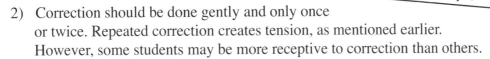

1)  Remember, often Beginners cannot hear their pronunciation mistakes.

   I remember when I was trying to learn the word "popular" in Spanish (po-pu-lar). I repeatedly said, "po-pyu-lar," and could not understand why my Venezuelan helper kept correcting me!

2)  Correction should be done gently and only once or twice. Repeated correction creates tension, as mentioned earlier. However, some students may be more receptive to correction than others.

3)  In the Student Workbook, you will use **Backward Build-up** to teach sentences:

   Teacher: "to the mountain." (Students repeat.)

   Teacher: "with your son to the mountain." (Students repeat.)

   Teacher: "Go with your son to the mountain." (Students repeat.)

   Breaking sentences into brief natural phrases and beginning at the end of the sentence makes it is easier for students to learn.

## G.  STUDENTS NEED THE FREEDOM TO *OCCASIONALLY* USE THEIR NATIVE LANGUAGE.

1)  This can be a major factor in reducing stress and creating a positive atmosphere. I have received much positive feedback from students for

---

* I am indebted to Howard Pollock for this illustration.

this approach. Many have complained of how uptight the "No Spanish in here!" approach has made them feel. I recommend that YOU don't feel uptight if they use their native language occasionally.

2) Use of their native language permits the freedom to ask questions and display humor.

3) The teacher can use the students' native language occasionally to give explanations or express humor. At times, a few words of explanation can save you a lot of time and energy!

4) Limits should be placed on the use of their native language.

   a) Do not say in their language what they can say in English.

   b) Do not ask constantly for translations.

5) As they are able, reduce the use of their native language in the classroom.

## H. A WARM AND ACCEPTING ATMOSPHERE IS VITAL TO SUCCESS.

1) Setting a pleasant atmosphere will help people feel welcome. This is especially true with people from different cultures where, in many cases, hospitality is a highly held value.

2) In my New Jersey classroom, I painted the walls, cleaned the rugs, and brought in tables, posters, a coffeepot and cookies.

   *Why?* Because teaching English is a ministry to people. As a ministry, it should be a relationship-builder, not simply a language class.

3) Your attitude toward the students, and their mistakes, is probably the most important "atmosphere setter" of all! Be patient.

## Guidelines for Using TPR Techniques

WEEK 1    WEEK 2    WEEK 3

### A. FEELING COMFORTABLE WITH TPR TAKES TIME.

I have mentioned the importance of being patient with the students. It is also important to be patient with yourself.

I remember observing Monique's first TPR class. What she had planned to take

45 minutes was over in 15 minutes. She stared at me with the expression, "Now what?" While the class took a coffee break, we talked about relaxing. She needed to try to think on her feet as she directed the students, instead of looking at notes after every sentence. She was hurrying through everything. She jumped back into it and after a few weeks was doing well.

### B. THINKING ON YOUR FEET IS NECESSARY IN USING TPR.

You cannot possibly write down beforehand every command you will give in class. As you become comfortable with how to direct the students, you will be able to be increasingly spontaneous. **Practice before your first class.** Practice giving commands to friends, other teachers or imaginary students. Practice will help you think on your feet later.

### C. THE SUCCESS OF EACH STUDENT, NOT COVERING THE LESSON, IS THE GOAL.

The pace of your lessons is determined by this. If students are not responding successfully, SLOW DOWN. Why proceed if they are failing? Keeping their success foremost in your mind will ensure their progress, lower anxiety and keep them motivated. If you ignore this guideline, the drop-out rate in your class *will* rise.

### D. DO NOT OVERUSE TPR.

1) TPR is fun, but as with any method it can be "run into the ground." Students may resist responding if TPR is used too often or for too long during class.

2) Use TPR in 15- to 25-minute time blocks. Alternate it with work on the alphabet, numbers, games, reading and writing exercises. Remember, TPR is only one of four components in the curriculum (see page xvii).

### E. FUNNY, CRAZY COMMANDS ARE TO BE ENCOURAGED!

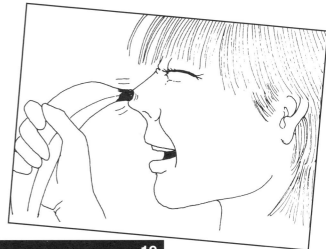

1) Doing some zany things stimulates better retention.

For example, "Scratch your nose with the banana."

2) It helps if you are a "ham," but it is not a prerequisite for using TPR. If you are not a "ham," maybe one or two of your students will be!

3) When giving zany commands, begin with yourself and use good taste. The idea is to enhance learning, not to embarrass people.

## Picture Review

Each picture illustrates a point about TPR or language learning. As a review, write a statement about the underlying principle of each picture. When you are finished, refer to previous pages to check your answers.

_____

_____

Page 10

_____

_____

Page 12

_____

_____

Page 14

_____

_____

Page 14

LEARN          USE IT

EARS BEFORE EYES

WEEK 1    WEEK 2    WEEK 3

# Introductory Techniques for TPR

When you first introduce an item, the techniques described below can be used. You will not use every one of them all of the time. Some techniques, such as "process of elimination" and "obvious command," you will use only occasionally.

The process of introducing items is a logical one:

**Model** &longrightarrow; **Together** &longrightarrow; **Hesitate** &longrightarrow; **Alone** &longrightarrow; **Jumble**

If you begin with **Alone,** the students will give you a blank stare. Why? Because the item is new, and they will not know what you are asking them to do! So, begin with **Model** and move on from there. You "observed" this process in the TPR classroom earlier in this chapter.

As your confidence grows, you will be able to use the techniques as needed or wanted. Let's look at this process in more detail.

## A. THE MODELING PROCESS

This technique is actually a "process of techniques" that begins with **Modeling** and ends with students performing **Alone.** Each step below is a technique in itself, but they can be combined into this process. This is the process you will use regularly in the Student Workbook.

Using hand gestures will help you communicate with students in the early stages. Before **Modeling,** give them the following instructions, accompanied with gestures.

| **Say:** | **"Listen** | **to** | **me."** |
|---|---|---|---|
| Do: | point to them | grab your ear | point to yourself |

| **Say:** | **"You** | **watch** | **me."** |
|---|---|---|---|
| Do: | point to them | point to your eye | point to yourself |

| **Say:** | **"Do not** | **speak."** | |
|---|---|---|---|
| Do: | wave finger negatively | point to your mouth | |

1) **Model:** Teacher performs, students observe.

   a) Teacher says, "Stand up. Sit down."

   b) Teacher, by herself, stands up and then sits down.

2) Before performing together,
   **Say:** **"Now,**      **together."**
   Do:    point to them      and yourself

   **Say:** **"Do not**      **speak."**
   Do:    wave finger negatively      point to your mouth

   **Together:** Teacher and student perform together.

   a) Teacher says, "Stand up. Sit down."

   b) Teacher and student stand up and sit down.

3) **Hesitate:** Teacher gives command but hesitates before performing.

   a) Teacher says, "Stand up. Sit down."

   b) Teacher waits to see if student begins to respond successfully, and then performs to reinforce the student's response.

4) Before they perform alone,
   **Say:** **"Now, you**      **alone."**
   Do:    point to them      point negatively to yourself

   **Alone:** Teacher gives command and student performs alone.

   a) Teacher says, "Stand up. Sit down."

   b) Only the student performs.

5) **Jumble:** Teacher gives commands in jumbled order. This is used especially **when a series of commands has been given in a set order.** For example, in Bible Sequence #1:

   | Normal | Jumbled |
   |---|---|
   | 1. Look at the apple tree. | 1. Grab an apple. |
   | 2. Walk to the tree. | 2. Walk to the tree. |
   | 3. Grab an apple. | 3. Look at the apple tree. |

   The **Jumble** technique is useful when doing the Bible Sequences because the actions are presented in a set order. By changing the set order, you check the students' comprehension. It can also be used with TPR commands.

a) Teacher says, "Sit down. Sit down. Stand up."

b) Student performs.

### B. PROCESS OF ELIMINATION

This is a technique you can use when introducing new objects, such as books, colors, fruit and so on. The student already knows an item. You then put a new item next to the familiar one. Through a process of elimination, the student will "guess" the new item.

1) For example:  The student already knows, "Touch the blue book."
The teacher puts a red book next to the blue book.
The student has not heard "red" before.
The teacher says, "Touch the red book."
The student realizes the other book must be "red."

### C. OBVIOUS COMMANDS

Here the teacher **Models** an initial command. The second command then becomes obvious.

1) For example:  The teacher performs with the student, saying,
"Open the door."
She then tells the student,
"Close the door."
The student guesses what "close" means.

Students are usually successful. If not, then **Model** for them.

2) This is helpful with opposites: open/close, on/off, hot/cold, wet/dry, soft/hard, right/left.

3) Gestures or pictures can be used to communicate the "obvious" meaning.

## Working Techniques for TPR

These techniques can come into play immediately after students begin performing commands. They help you "work" the new items and are used in review as well. **Chain Commands, Connectives** and **Recombining** are used from the very first day of class. The other techniques, **More Complicated Settings, Cue Cards** and **Problem Solving,** are used after students have mastered the vocabulary.

## A. CHAIN COMMANDS

This technique can be used with **Model, Together** and **Alone.** The teacher you "observed" used **Chain Commands** and **Connectives** on the first day of class.

1) Example: "Stand up. Sit down."

 "Stand up. Walk. Stop. Sit down."

 "Stand up. Walk. Stop. Turn around."

The teacher was **Chaining Commands** together.

2) Pause after each command and let the student perform.

3) Progressively, give them two, three or four commands at once. They listen to all the commands before performing. Show them two, three or four fingers and gesture for them to listen to all the commands before performing.

4) This technique "stretches" comprehension.

5) Gradually expand the number of commands from two up to four or five, but not beyond that. Remember, you want them to succeed, not fail.

6) This technique can also be used "in reverse." Give yourself four or five commands. If you perform them correctly, the students answer "right." If you make a mistake, they answer "wrong."

## B. CONNECTIVES (and, that is, then, now, after, before, while)

This technique naturally follows **Chain Command** and uses more normal speech patterns. Begin with the **Connective** "and." Use "and" for at least a week or two. Any new connective you introduce needs to be demonstrated first. Do not introduce more than one connective at a time. The Bible Sequences contain several connectives.

1) Example: "Go to the board and touch the board twice."

 "Turn around slowly and sit down."

 "Pick up the apple that is on the table."

## C. RECOMBINE

1) This technique is very important. The basic idea is to **Recombine** a new item students are learning with previous material before teaching another new item. Mix the new item with the old before adding more new items

(much like baking a cake by adding one ingredient at a time). If you introduce the verb "scratch," do so by using it first with vocabulary the students already know.

2) You can employ any number of techniques in order to **Recombine.**

As in the example, you are introducing, "scratch." You have **Modeled** and performed **Together.** Only the word "scratch" is new.

You can **Recombine** by using:

a) **Chain Command:**   "Stand up. Scratch the book. Scratch the table."

b) **Connective:**   "Stand up and scratch the table."

c) **More Complicated:**   "Scratch the book that is on the table."

d) **Role Reversal:**   Put several familiar verbs along with "scratch" on a cue card. The student must use them in a command.

3) **Recombining** prevents overwhelming the students with too much new material at once.

4) When introducing a new item, **Recombine** it with some familiar items and then practice for several minutes until they demonstrate confidence in responding to the new item. This allows students to learn a new item in "comfortable surroundings"—words they already know.

5) Another example:

a) **Alone:**   "Juan, touch the table." (familiar)

b) **Model:**   "Teacher, don't touch the table, point to the table." (Teacher gives command to herself and models.)

c) **Together:**   "Juan, point to the table."

d) **Alone:**   "Juan, turn around slowly (familiar) and point to the table." (The only new word for Juan is "point.")

6) The opposite approach to **Recombining** would be to introduce "point to" and then immediately begin pointing to a dozen new items in the room. That would be too much new information at once.

### D. NOVELTIES

1) A novelty is any **new combination** or **new situation** of language use. It

does not have to include new material, as with **Recombining,** but rather new combinations. Any new combination of places, people, commands or objects is a "novelty."

2) Example: "Touch your mouth. Open the door." (familiar)

"Open your mouth. Touch the door." (new)

3) Novelties are occurring frequently in the TPR classroom.

4) Novelties are the essence of communication. We do not repeat what we hear in order to communicate. Rather, we create new sentences to express ourselves.

## E. PUTTING COMMANDS IN MORE COMPLICATED SETTINGS
The goal here is to help students understand more complicated speech. In general, using a variety of **Connectives** is a good way to put familiar language into a more complicated setting.
1) Example: "Pick up the apple." (familiar)
"Put the apple in the basket." (familiar)
"Pick up the apple that is in the basket." (new)

"Scratch your head." (familiar)
"Scratch your head with the banana." (familiar)
"Put the banana in the basket." (familiar)
"Scratch your head with the banana that is in the basket."(new)

2) Experiment with making up commands. As long as the items are known to the students, the new combinations will not overwhelm them.

## F. ROLE REVERSAL
Students give commands to the teacher or others. This technique should not be used in the first week or two. Students need time to experience success in performing before you ask them to give commands. Do not expect them to jump right into **Role Reversal** after hearing a new item.

1) Student says, "Stand up. Sit down."

2) Teacher or another student performs.

Once students are comfortable with **Role Reversal,** you will be able to use **Cue Cards, Problem Solving, Pictures** and other objects to prompt them in using the language.

## G. CUE CARDS AND PICTURES

**Cue Cards** are very helpful for working the language and review.

1) Flash one or more verb **Cue Cards** from a previous lesson to a student or small group. They then direct others using that verb.

2) Give a group of students four to six **Cue Cards.** They write or orally give a series of commands to others, using the vocabulary on the cards.

3) From action **Pictures,** students can make up and use **Cue Cards** to direct others. For example, show them a **Picture** of a boy picking up a box and carrying it. They make up **Cue Cards** with the verbs "pick up" and "carry" on them and then direct others using those verbs.

## H. PROBLEM SOLVING

This technique has several purposes. One is to relate the content of class to real-life situations. It also makes students work together to create language. They must write several sentences that solve the problem and perform the solution. Give them any extra vocabulary they may need, but not too much — three or four items is about right. An example of a "problem": Tell a friend how to wash his hands and face.

## I. CREATING THEIR OWN SKITS

The students create their own skits using either vocabulary you give them or choosing their own from previous lessons.

# TPR Review

## Quick Reference for TPR Techniques

**Teachers:** Photocopy this page and keep as a quick reference for classroom use.

**MODEL**

**TOGETHER**

**HESITATE**

**ALONE**

**JUMBLE**

**ROLE REVERSAL**

**PROCESS OF ELIMINATION**

**OBVIOUS COMMANDS**

**CHAIN COMMANDS**

**CONNECTIVES**

**RECOMBINE (NEW WITH OLD)**

**NOVELTIES**

**MORE COMPLICATED SETTINGS**

**CUE CARDS AND PICTURES**

**PROBLEM SOLVING**

**SKITS**

# TPR Technique Review

**Teachers:** Write the name of the technique in the space provided. Choose from the following techniques: **Connectives, Chain Commands, Role Reversal, Recombine, Novelty, More Complicated, Cue Card, Problem Solving.**

_____ 1. "Stand up. Turn around. Walk. Stop."

_____ 2. "Point to the table. Point to the book." (familiar)
"Point to the book that is on the table." (new)

_____ 3. "Explain to a child how to plant a seed."

_____ 4. "Look at these cards and give commands."

_____ 5. "Pick up the bag. Close the box." (familiar)
"Close the bag. Pick up the box." (new)

_____ 6. A student tells another student, "Pick up the book. Open the book."

_____ 7. "Walk slowly." (familiar)
"Stop." (familiar)
"Scratch your nose." (new)
"Sit down." (familiar)

_____ 8. Point to the window and close the door.

**Answers:** 1) Chain, 2) More Complicated, 3) Problem Solving, 4) Cue Card, 5) Novelty, 6) Role Reversal, 7) Recombine, 8) Connective.

## Review Questions (answers on page 33)

**A. WHY DO WE SAY "DIRECT" LANGUAGE GROUPS INSTEAD OF "TEACH" THEM?**


**B. TPR IS BASED ON: _____**
1) memorizing stories
2) learning grammar
3) how children learn
4) telling stories

**C. TPR EMPHASIZES: _____**
1) body movement
2) listening
3) commands
4) explaining
5) all of the above

**D. GIVE ONE REASON WHY USING COMMANDS IS HELPFUL.**


**E. HOW IS INTERNALIZING DIFFERENT FROM MEMORIZING?**


**F. TPR LOWERS _____ FOR STUDENTS. _____ IS A MAJOR OBSTACLE TO LEARNING.**


**G. LEARN A _____ AND _____ IT _____.**

H.  THE FIRST TARGET OF TPR IS THE _____, NOT THE EYES.

I.  WHAT SHOULD OUR ATTITUDE BE TOWARD MISTAKES? WHY?

J.  THE S __ __ __ __ __ __ OF EACH STUDENT IS THE GOAL.

K.  WHY IS IT GOOD TO INCLUDE FUNNY OR CRAZY COMMANDS?

L.  PUT THE FOLLOWING IN LOGICAL ORDER:

| *INCORRECT:* | *CORRECT:* |
|---|---|
| **Model** | _____ |
| **Role Reversal** | _____ |
| **Hesitate** | _____ |
| do **Together** | _____ |
| student performs **Alone** | _____ |

M.  WHAT DOES "RECOMBINE" MEAN?

N.  RATHER THAN EXPLAIN THE LANGUAGE, YOU SHOULD TRY TO

D __ __ __ __ __ __ __ __ __ __

AND I __ __ __ __ __ __ THE STUDENTS.

# Answers to Review Questions

A. Our role is to direct the action, not explain the language.

B. 3) how children learn

C. 1) body movement; 2) listening; 3) commands

D. Frequency of use in daily life; 40% of work vocabulary; gets people moving; easy to use; form the base of verbs.

E. Internalizing focuses on using the language in creative ways, while memorizing is recalling a copy of something.

F. anxiety; anxiety

G. little, use, a lot

H. ears

I. Patience, because mistakes are inevitable and demonstrating patience will lower anxiety for the students.

J. Success

K. It helps long-term retention.

L. **Model**

   **Together**

   **Hesitate**

   **Alone**

   **Role Reversal**

M. When introducing a new item, first use it with previously taught vocabulary before introducing more new items.

N. demonstrate, involve

OPTIONAL

# Teaching Other Items

Chapter

2

# The Alphabet

When teaching the alphabet, the literacy level and native language of your students will determine how fast you can go; see "Placement Test" in Chapter 3 for student levels. With True Beginners, introduce only one or two items at a time. With False Beginners, you can introduce three to five items. Let their success be your guide. For students who are unfamiliar with the English alphabet, it is important to go more slowly. With these students, take time to demonstrate exactly how each letter is traced. Provide time to practice forming the letters. Be certain to incorporate the letters as part of daily review and TPR work.

## A. PROCEDURE

1) Recite in order three to five letters as students listen.

2) Recite the letters randomly, as students listen.

3) Recite the letters randomly as you point to them. Students say "yes" or "no" after each letter they hear.

4) Go around the room with each student reciting a letter in order.

5) Go around the room with each student reciting the letter you indicate.

6) Dictate 3 to 5 letters at normal speed.

## B. GAMES TO PLAY WITH THE ALPHABET

1) Students stand up when they hear their name being spelled.

2) Play "Hangman," using lesson vocabulary.

3) Write commands they know on the board, leaving blanks; they fill in the blanks orally or write at the board.

   For example: "P_ _k  _p  th_  bo_k."

4) "TPR" the alphabet cards.

   For example: "Put *C* under *J*. Touch *P*."

5) Spell words as they are dictated using "position words" (prepositions) they have learned.

   For example, dictate "walk" in the following manner: "Write *a;* to the left of the *a,* write *w;* to the right of the *a,* write *l;* to the right of the *l,* write *k.*"

This can also be done in *crossword* fashion.

6) Write home addresses.

7) Have students dictate their first, middle and last names for other students to write.

8) Play TPR Bingo (available from Sky Oaks Productions, Inc; see page xi to order).

9) Point to familiar body parts, colors or items and ask students to spell them.

# Numbers

## A. PROCEDURE

1) Recite numbers in order, using fingers, the chalkboard or cards.

2) Recite numbers randomly.

3) Recite numbers randomly as you point to them. Students say "yes" or "no."

4) Recite, pause, then show the number.

5) Go around the room with each student reciting a number in order.

6) Go around the room with each student reciting random numbers you indicate.

7) Dictate 3 to 5 numbers at normal speed.

8) Use **Cue Cards** for higher numbers.

## B. GAMES TO PLAY WITH NUMBERS

1) Telephone numbers (practice proper "pause"). Recite student phone numbers. Students stand up when they recognize their own number.

2) Roll dice; students add out loud and announce total.

3) Contrast numbers; point to a number and say, "Is it 5 or 15?"

4) Teacher says, "I am thinking of a number. It is higher than 17. Is it 11 or 18?"

5) Count aloud by 2s, 3s, 5s or 10s.

6) Use a stopwatch and have students compete in counting.

7) Do simple math problems; students recite the problem and the answer (3 + 3 = 6; three, plus, three, equals, six).

8) Guess each other's height by teams, how much loose change each has on them, or how long it would take them to walk home.

## C. LETTERS AND NUMBERS TOGETHER

1) Recite and/or write addresses.

2) Recite and/or write license plates.

3) Recite and/or write birth dates.

4) Recite days of the week and months of the year; introduce and practice as with the alphabet.

5) Recite numbered dates (3/12/96); students must write or spell name dates (March twelfth, nineteen ninety-six) and vice-versa.

# Telling Time

1) Practice digital times such as 9:20 or 10:15.

2) Practice position words: past, after, before, of, 'til.

3) Practice other time terms: quarter, half, o'clock.

4) Show the class 2:30 as if your arms are a clock's hands.

5) Use props found at educational materials stores for teaching time.

# Simon Says

## A. BODY PARTS

1) Play "Simon Says," by teams or individually, using TPR verbs with the body (touch, point to, etc.).

2) Point to body parts and have students spell them.

## B. TPR COMMANDS

1) Play "Simon Says" with TPR commands. If students respond incorrectly, they are out of the game.

# Greetings, Leave-takings and Expressions of Gratitude

Some of your beginning students will be False Beginners; that is, they actually know some English and are able to say simple greetings and leave-takings. However, you will also have True Beginners who know almost nothing. (See Chapter 3, "Placement Test," for more information on skill levels.) I recommend that you include in your second and third weeks of class some work on greetings and leave-takings. If you speak the language of your students, explain some of the differences in the exchanges as you teach them.

Also feel free to add other simple exchanges to this list. First, model the exchange yourself several times. Then write one sentence at a time on the board and practice pronunciation together using **Backward Build-up.**

When students have gained confidence in saying the sentences, practice the exchanges **Together** with the entire class. Continue with several individuals, changing roles.

Ask willing students to do an exchange **Alone** as the rest of the class observes. After a few exchanges have been learned, practice can take place in groups. Also, make practicing greetings and leave-takings a regular part of your class as students come and go.

## A. GREETINGS

Greeting #1
Student 1: "Hello. How are you today?"
Student 2: "Fine, thanks. And you?"
Student 1: "Fine."

Greeting #2
Student 1: "Hello (Hi), my name is _____."
Student 2: "Hello (Hi), my name is _____."
Student 1: "Nice to meet you."
Student 2: "Nice to meet you, too."

## B. LEAVE-TAKINGS

Leave-taking #1
    Student 1: "Have a nice day."
    Student 2: "Thanks. Same to you."

Leave-taking #2
    Student 1: "Nice meeting you."
    Student 2: "Same to you."
    Student 1: "Good-bye."
    Student 2: "Good-bye."

## C. EXPRESSIONS OF GRATITUDE

    Student 1: "Thank you."
    Student 2: "You're welcome."

*Other Expressions of Gratitude*

    "Thanks for your help."
    "Thanks very much."
    "Thanks a lot."

# Survival Texts

Sometimes students are eager to "converse" with English speakers from day one of their language-learning experience. Introducing Survival Texts is an option you can use with students to supplement your work in the curriculum. A text should be learned, practiced and used over a period of days.

## A. SAMPLE SURVIVAL TEXTS

**Text # 1**

1. "Hello. My name is _____."
2. "I am learning English."
3. "This is all I can say right now."
4. "I will learn more soon."
5. "Thanks for listening to me."

**Text # 2**

1. "Hello. How are you?"
2. "My name is _____."
3. "What is your name?"
4. "I am learning English."
5. "I want to speak well."
6. "Thanks for listening to me."
7. "Good-bye."

**Text # 3**

1. "Hello."
2. "I am learning English."
3. "My name is _____."
4. "What's your name?"
5. "What is this?"
6. "How much does this cost?"
7. "Thank you."
8. "Good-bye."

**Text # 4**

1. "Hello."
2. "I am learning English."
3. "Where is _____?"
4. "Is it close by?"
5. "Can I walk there?"
6. "Thank you."
7. "Good-bye."

## B. HOW TO TEACH A SURVIVAL TEXT*

1. If possible, have a native speaker explain the text to the students. If that is not possible, "TPR" as much of the text as possible. By using TPR, gestures and mimicking, students should grasp the meaning of the text.

2. Use **Backward Build-up** to help students master the pronunciation of the text. This will require a significant amount of time and repetition.

3. Practice the text in class. Go from group to group encouraging and correcting.

4. Encourage students to use the text outside of class.

## C. HOW TO SOLICIT A SURVIVAL TEXT FROM THE STUDENTS

1. What do the students want or need to learn to say?

2. Have them write a text (five to eight lines) in their native language.

3. Have someone translate the *meaning* (not word-for-word) of the text into English.

4. Follow the steps above to teach the text.

---

*I am indebted to Dr. Betty Sue Brewster for teaching me to use Survival Texts as I learned Spanish.

# Teaching Questions

Questions should be introduced to work with vocabulary the students have already learned. Following are some suggestions for teaching questions.

**A. ASK THE QUESTION TO YOURSELF AND "MODEL" AN ANSWER SEVERAL TIMES.** You may need to use gestures and explanations to help students understand the question.

**B. ASK STUDENTS THE QUESTION SEVERAL TIMES TO CHECK COMPREHENSION.** Do not expect complete-sentence answers. Do they understand the question?

**C. DO "BACKWARD BUILD-UP"** to help students produce the question. For example, the question is:

"What are you doing?"

1) Repeat: "doing?"

2) Repeat: "are you doing?"

3) Repeat: "What are you doing?"

**D. USE PROPS** to solicit questions and responses from the students. For example:

1) The teacher points to a shoe and calls on Jose. Jose picks up the shoe and asks Maria, "What is this?"

2) The teacher points to the window as a cue to Maria. Maria tells Jose to point to the window. While Jose is pointing to the window, Maria asks him, "What are you doing?"

**E. CONTINUE PRACTICING FOR SEVERAL MINUTES** as a class or in groups. Remember, always **Recombine** once a new item is understood. Instead of asking the same question in isolation over and over again, try recombining it with previous material. For example,

"Jorge, stand up, touch the table with your nose, turn around slowly and ask Teresa, 'What are you doing?' "

**F. INCORPORATE THE QUESTION INTO YOUR TPR WORK,** once the students have demonstrated success in understanding and using the question. For example, after teaching them the question, "Can you _____?," you then ask a student, "Can you stand up?" "Yes." "Good. Then stand up!"

**G. USE CUE CARDS** of verbs or vocabulary to prompt questions. This is good practice. For example, the teacher holds up a cue card that says, "Hit." A student needs to ask a familiar question incorporating the word "hit." This can be used as a game in groups.

**H. SLOW DOWN** if, at any point, you sense the students are overwhelmed with the questions. After they are confident in using a question, then a new one may be introduced.

# Designing Your Own TPR Lessons

Once you feel comfortable and confident in using TPR, it is simple to begin designing your own lessons. The lessons can take place either in a secular or biblical setting, whichever best suits your purpose.

Suppose that you want to design a lesson for an everyday activity, such as washing your hands.

## A. SUGGESTED STEPS

**STEP 1:** Visualize the setting and the specific movements needed to perform the activity. Then frame the activity into eight to 12 simple action lines. One caution: In your effort to keep the language simple, do not write action lines that are incorrect grammatically. For example, do not write, "Dry face with towel." Write instead, "Dry your face with the towel." Adjust the difficulty of the action lines to the level appropriate for your students. Adding items such as descriptive words increases the difficulty level. For example, "Dry your face quickly with the thick towel."

### WASHING YOUR HANDS (sample text)

1. Your hands are dirty.
2. Go to the sink.
3. Turn on the water.
4. Pick up the soap.
5. Wash your hands.
6. Put the soap down.
7. Rinse your hands.
8. Turn off the water.

9. Pick up the towel.

10. Dry your hands.

11. Hang the towel on the hook.

**STEP 2:** Separate the vocabulary into three lists: verbs, nouns, other.

**Verbs:** are, go to, turn (on), pick (up), wash, put (down), rinse, turn (off), dry, hang

**Nouns:** hands, sink, water, soap, towel, hook

**Other:** the, your

**STEP 3:** TPR some of the vocabulary before teaching the newly created sequence. How much? Leave no more than six to eight new items in a sequence before you teach it. In the new sequence, "Washing Your Hands," if all of the vocabulary (about 17 items) is new to the students, then you should TPR at least half of the vocabulary before beginning. Students should be able to learn the other vocabulary items from the context of the story. However, if you prefer, it would be fine to TPR all of the new items before beginning.

**STEP 4:** Teach the sequence using the step-by-step procedure instructions given in Chapter 5.

**STEP 5:** Draw upon the Expansion Activities listed in Chapter 5 to expand student abilities.

## B. SOME SUGGESTED ACTIVITIES FOR TPR SEQUENCES

| **Household** | **Classroom** | **Body** |
|---|---|---|
| making a sandwich | tying your shoes | shaving |
| preparing breakfast | wrapping a present | putting on make-up |
| washing dishes | making a paper airplane | shampooing/combing hair |
| making a bed | threading a needle | doing stretching exercises |
| setting the table | drawing a picture | putting on suntan lotion |
| feeding a baby | sharpening a pencil | putting on jewelry |

# Classroom Helps and Handouts

# Pre-Course Questionnaire

(Note to teachers: This form is to be translated and distributed to each student in his or her primary language.)

Name_____ Address_____

1. How long have you lived in the U.S.A.? _____

2. What is the highest level of education you have completed?

    ___ Elementary    ___ High School    ___ University

3. For what communicative situations and tasks do you wish to learn English? Put in order of priority.

    ___    A. talking in formal situations (doctor, post office, etc.)

    ___    B. understanding the radio and television

    ___    C. filling in forms

    ___    D. understanding native speakers

    ___    E. reading the newspaper

    ___    F. understanding the American way of life

    ___    G. writing letters

    ___    H. talking to friends and neighbors

    ___    I. improve academics

4. Which skills are most important to you? Put in order of priority.

    ___    A. speaking

    ___    B. listening

    ___    C. writing

    ___    D. reading

# Placement Test

The purpose of this test is to help the teacher decide where students should begin in the curriculum. Testing of this nature can be quite subjective. When in doubt, place the student at the earlier starting point. Start Beginners at Lesson 1 and HiBeginners at Lesson 4. Start HiBeginners/LowIntermediates at Lesson 4 and then skip to Lesson 8.

## STUDENT LEVELS

**True Beginners & English-alphabet–Illiterate:** Extremely limited comprehension and verbal ability. Know only a few dozen words, if any.

**False Beginners & Literate Beginners:** Very limited in comprehension and verbal ability. Often know simple greetings and leave-takings, as well as numbers and the alphabet. May be able to read some in English.

**HiBeginners:** Can communicate with survival vocabulary in such areas as food, money, clothes, transportation, greetings and questions. However, grammar is poor and vocabulary is limited.

**LowIntermediates:** Communicate fairly well, often in complete sentences but with frequent grammatical errors. Conversation range is greater than HiBeginners but is still limited. Have difficulty forming questions.

Student Name _____

Address _____

Phone _____

Start curriculum at:    ____ Lesson 1

                            ____ Lesson 4

                            ____ Lessons 4 and 8

Interviewer _____     Date _____

**COMPREHENSION** (props: chair, table, book, pencil)
Read aloud and mark student's response.

Correct    Incorrect

| Correct | Incorrect | |
|---|---|---|
| _____ | _____ | 1. Stand up. Sit down. |
| _____ | _____ | 2. Touch the table. |
| _____ | _____ | 3. Close your eyes. |
| _____ | _____ | 4. Put your finger on your nose. |
| _____ | _____ | 5. Touch the book. |
| _____ | _____ | 6. Put the pencil on the book. |
| _____ | _____ | 7. Give the pencil to me. |
| _____ | _____ | 8. Put the pencil under the book. |
| _____ | _____ | 9. Point to the book. |
| _____ | _____ | 10. Point to the floor. |
| _____ | _____ | 11. Stand up, turn around and sit down. |
| _____ | _____ | 12. Pick up the book. |
| _____ | _____ | 13. Hold the book and pick up the pencil. |
| _____ | _____ | 14. Smell the book. |
| _____ | _____ | 15. Put your hand between the book and the pencil. |
| _____ | _____ | 16. Scratch the table. |
| _____ | _____ | 17. Don't stand up. Put your hand on the table. |
| _____ | _____ | 18. Touch your head. |
| _____ | _____ | 19. Put the pencil inside the book. |
| _____ | _____ | 20. Look at the floor. |

SCORE:   ___ Beginner = fewer than 10 correct

           ___ Moderate/HiBeginner = 10–15 correct

           ___ HiBeginner/LowIntermediate = 15–20 correct

**ALPHABET** (Students recite each letter in order and then randomly. Fewer than 80% correct = Beginner.)

A B C D E F G H I J K L M N O P Q R S T U V W X Y Z

**NUMBERS** (Student recites each number in order, then randomly. Fewer than 80% correct = Beginner.)

1 2 3 4 5 6 7 8 9 10 11 12 13 14 15 16 17 18 19 20 30 40 50 60 70 80 90 100

**CONVERSATION** (Great difficulty = Beginner.)

|  | Great difficulty | Moderate or less difficulty |
|---|---|---|
| 1. What is your name? |  |  |
| 2. Where are you from? |  |  |
| 3. How long have you lived in _____? |  |  |
| 4. What is your address? |  |  |
| 5. When is your birthday? |  |  |
| 6. What is your occupation? |  |  |
| 7. What time is it? |  |  |
| 8. What is your nationality? |  |  |
| 9. What language do you speak? |  |  |
| 10. Why do you want to learn English? |  |  |

# Lesson Planning

(Note to teachers: The following three pages are helpful if you design your own TPR lessons.)

If you want to include the alphabet, numbers and other items in your class, this page will give you a feel for planning a lesson.

Use the overview section of the Lesson Plan Worksheet on the following page to organize the content for the class. Think in terms of 5- to 15-minute time slots for special items such as alphabet, numbers and games. TPR practice goes well in 15- to 25-minute slots. In general, do not work on TPR for more than 25 minutes without a change of pace, or you will wear out yourself and the students. However, do not be a prisoner of time slots either. If an activity is going well, feel free to keep it going. When you do not cover everything in the lesson plan, just note where you left off and start the next lesson there. Plan to always spend at least 10 minutes every class meeting reviewing things covered earlier.

It is a good idea to have variety in the way you conduct the class. Do not do the same things every day in the same order. Below is a basic lesson-plan approach you can use for a 2-hour class. Change the order when you think appropriate.

| | |
|---|---|
| 15 minutes | 1. Review previous TPR |
| 10 minutes | 2. Numbers (or a game) |
| 20–25 minutes | 3. New TPR verbs/vocabulary |
| 10 minutes | 4. Break |
| 10 minutes | 5. Alphabet (or a game) |
| 20–25 minutes | 6. New TPR verbs/vocabulary |
| 10 minutes | 7. Question/game or recombine day's commands |
| 15 minutes | 8. Lesson summary |

# Lesson Plan Worksheet #_____

(Note to teachers: Photocopy for your own use if designing your own TPR lessons.)

**VOCABULARY:**

   **Verbs:**


   **Nouns:**


   **Other:**

**PROPS:**_____

_____


**HANDOUTS:**_____

_____


**OVERVIEW OF CLASS PERIOD**

| Estimated Time | Topic | Notes |
|---|---|---|
| _____ | 1. _____ | |
| _____ | 3. _____ | |
| _____ | 4. _____ | |
| _____ | 5. _____ | |
| _____ | 6. _____ | |
| _____ | 7. _____ | |
| _____ | 8. _____ | |
| _____ | 9. _____ | |
| _____ | 10. _____ | |

# Lesson Summary Worksheet #_____

(Note to teachers: If designing your own TPR lessons, photocopy one for **each** student before **each** class.)

| VERBS | NOUNS | OTHER |
| --- | --- | --- |

**SAMPLE SENTENCES:**

# Testing Your Students

A. **WHAT YOU SEE IS WHAT YOU GET!** Every day you will see the students' comprehension demonstrated through TPR.

B. **MANY OF THE ITEMS FROM THE EXPANSION ACTIVITIES CAN BE USED AS TESTS** to check comprehension, reading and writing. For example:

1) Change the tense (present to present continuous, etc.).

2) Ask questions about the Bible Sequence.

3) Use cue cards to prompt students; they perform what the card says. Award one point for each correct response.

4) Show cue cards that have the beginning of a question on them. For example, "Can you_____?" The students must ask correct questions.

C. **FILL IN THE BLANKS.** Use with commands and individual words.

D. **GIVE A SERIES OF 10 COMMANDS.**
Credit one point for each one completed correctly.

E. **SENTENCE COMPLETION.** "Jorge, go to_____ and_____."

F. **MULTIPLE CHOICE.** *The Graphics Book,* by Ramiro Garcia, Sky Oaks Productions, Inc., contains multiple-choice tests for TPR students (see page xi).

G. **RECITE A SERIES OF FOUR TO FIVE COMMANDS.** Then perform them yourself while the students observe. If you complete them exactly as you recited them, the students write "yes." If you err in the slightest detail, the students write "no." Award points for correct responses.

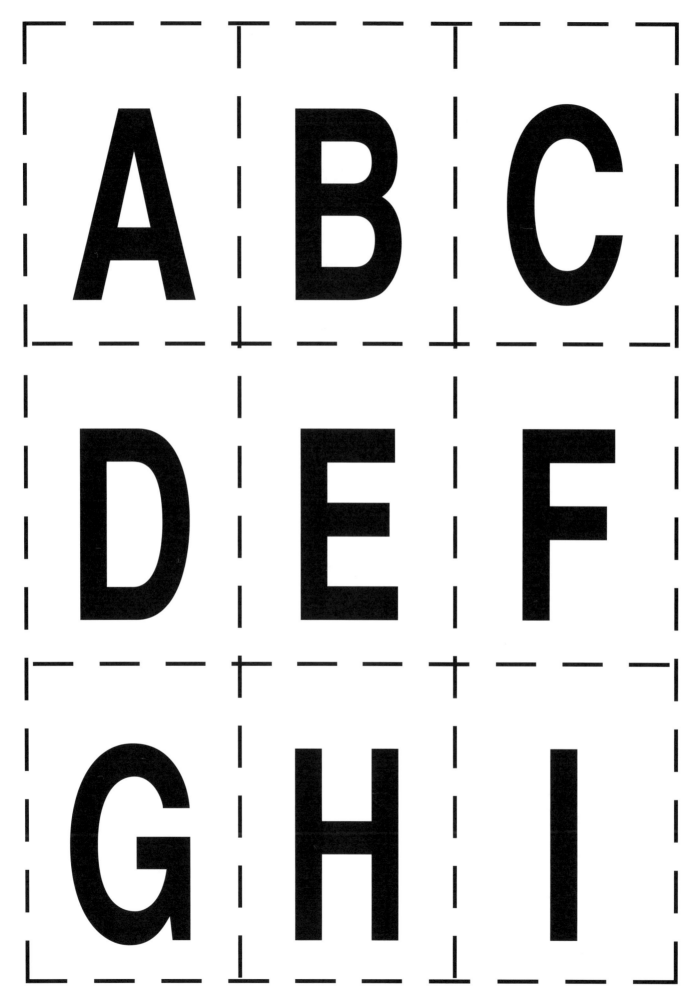

54

| J | K | L |
|---|---|---|
| M | N | O |
| P | Q | R |

S T U

V W X

Y Z

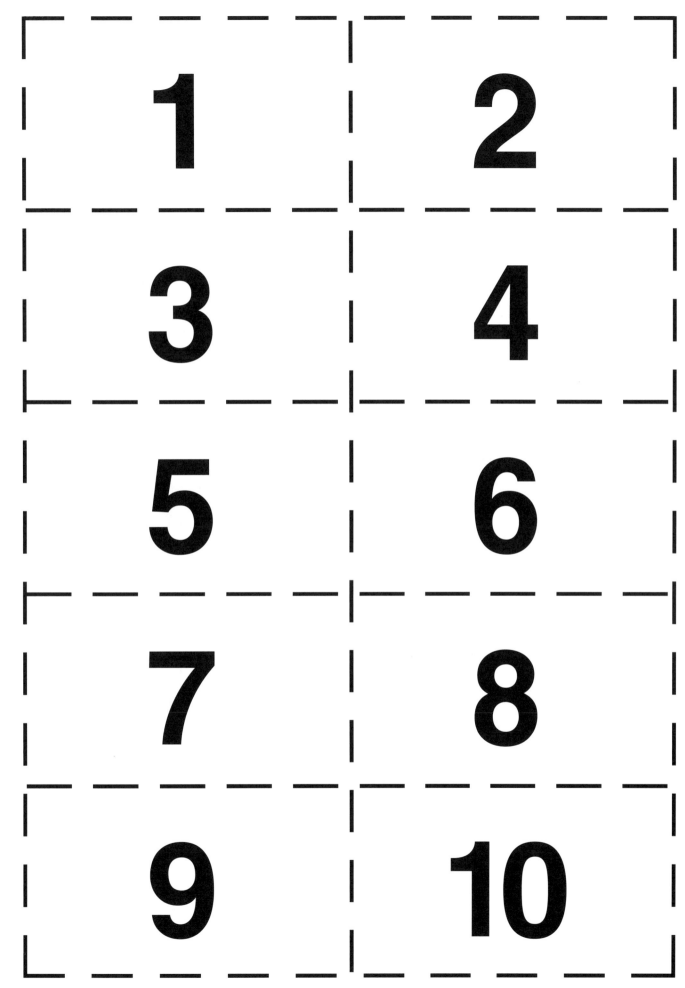

| 11 | 12 |
|:--:|:--:|
| 13 | 14 |
| 15 | 16 |
| 17 | 18 |
| 19 | 20 |

| 10 | 20 |
|:---:|:---:|
| 30 | 40 |
| 50 | 60 |
| 70 | 80 |
| 90 | 100 |

SUNDAY

MONDAY

TUESDAY

WEDNESDAY

THURSDAY

FRIDAY

SATURDAY

| SUNDAY | MONDAY | TUESDAY | WEDNESDAY | THURSDAY | FRIDAY | SATURDAY |
|--------|--------|---------|-----------|----------|--------|----------|
|  |  | 3 | 4 | 5 | 6 | 7 |
| 8 | 9 | 10 | 11 | 12 | 13 | 14 |
| 15 | 16 | 17 | 18 | 19 | 20 | 21 |
| 22 | 23 | 24 | 25 | 26 | 27 | 28 |
| 29 | 30 |  |  |  |  |  |

61

| JANUARY | FEBRUARY |
|---------|----------|
| MARCH | APRIL |
| MAY | JUNE |
| JULY | AUGUST |
| SEPTEMBER | OCTOBER |
| NOVEMBER | DECEMBER |

# Teacher's Guide for the Student Workbook

B

# Overview of the Student Workbook

Chapter 4

# Introduction

Following is an overview of the content of the Student Workbook, *English In Action.* The Student Workbook has two purposes. One is to teach English, and the other is to move people toward a personal relationship with Christ.

The spiritual impact of the Student Workbook lies: **(1)** in learning the Bible Sequences, and **(2)** in the Reading Section, where students are taken directly into the Bible and the discussion of spiritual truths. Additional verses and a discussion question for each Bible passage is provided in the Lesson Plans for each Bible Sequence (Chapter 7).

The Bible Sequences involve the students physically in a biblical event. This will impact their long-term memory. It also sets the stage, not only for language learning but also for the discussion of the event.

**The Reading Section is included primarily for spiritual impact and secondarily for language growth.** Thus, if for whatever reason the students are not able to understand the exercise in English, look for a way to use it with them in their native tongue.

# The Beginning Lessons

This is the starting point for the Student Workbook. These lessons lay the vocabulary foundation needed by the students to master the Bible Sequences. A large portion of the vocabulary found in the sequences is learned in these early lessons. Beyond helping students internalize vocabulary, the students also will begin to feel comfortable with TPR and learn such basics as the alphabet, numbers, colors and questions.

The detailed lesson plans for the Beginning Lessons begin in Chapter 6.

# The Biblical Content of the Sequences

The Old Testament sequences are designed to be a springboard for a prophetic view of the coming Messiah. The Bible Sequence events are not prophetic in themselves but the characters involved (Adam and Eve, Abraham, Moses, David and Jonah) represent a link in Messianic prophecy.

The New Testament sequences give a simple overview of the life of Christ.

Biblical events that could be made to work in a TPR sequence were chosen. The reading section leads students to the actual Bible passage from which the sequence was derived. A discussion question and additional verses are provided in the Teacher's Lesson Plans for each Bible Sequence.

## PROPHETIC LINKS OF THE OLD TESTAMENT SEQUENCES

| Sequence # | Topic |
|---|---|
| 1 | Adam and Eve: The Messiah Will Come through the Human Race (Genesis 3:15) |
| 2 | Abraham: The Messiah Will Come through the Nation of Israel (Genesis 12:1–3) |
| 3 | Moses: The Messiah Will Be a Prophet Who Comes through the Tribe of Judah (Deuteronomy 18:15 and Genesis 49:10) |
| 4 | David: The Messiah Will Come through the Family of David (2 Samuel 7:14) |
| 5 | Jonah: The Messiah Will Fulfill the Sign of Jonah (Matthew 12:38–40) |

## NEW TESTAMENT SEQUENCES

| Sequence # | Topic |
|---|---|
| 6 | Jesus' Birth: Wise Men Visit (Matthew 2:1–11) |
| 7 | Miracle: Wedding at Cana (John 2:1–11) |
| 8 | Miracle: Feeding of the 5,000 (John 6:5–14) |
| 9 | Miracle: Healing of a Blind Man (John 9:1–15) |
| 10 | Parable: The Sower (Mark 4:3–8) |
| 11 | Parable: The Lost Coin (Luke 15:8–9) |
| 12 | Parable: The Hidden Treasure (Matthew 13:44) |
| 13 | Parable: The Good Samaritan (Luke 10:30–37) |
| 14 | Jesus Is Crucified (Luke 23:26–46) |
| 15 | The Empty Tomb (John 20:1–9) |

## The Purpose of Each Section of the Student Workbook

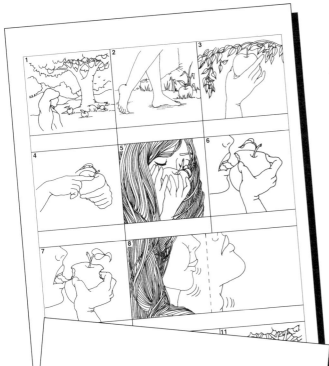

Adam and Eve

**Genesis 3:1-6**

1. Look at the apple tree.
2. Walk to the tree.
3. Grab an apple.
4. Feel the apple.
5. Smell it.
6. Take a bite.
7. Take another bite.
8. Chew and swallow.
9. You feel sad.
10. Throw away the apple.
11. Hide behind the tree.

### A. THE PICTURES

1) The pictures are an excellent tool for practicing TPR and building vocabulary. Make it a habit to TPR the sequence pictures. For example, "Point to the apple." "Don't touch the apple. Touch the tree." "Put your finger on 'swallow.'"

2) Pictures are at the beginning of each chapter so that the focus is on them, not on reading the text. They are also used extensively in Expansion Activities.

3) Look for creative ways to use the pictures. For example, with children, make photocopies and have them color the pictures.

### B. THE TYPED TEXT

1) This section provides a clear copy of the text.

2) It provides the "answers" for the Word Order and Fill-in-the-Blank exercises. If students have difficulty with either of these exercises, all they need to do is look at the typed text for the answers.

3) This section provides a place for students to write notations about words and phrases.

## C. THE PRONUNCIATION SECTION

This part is included because students often want help with pronunciation. Each chapter highlights two English vowel sounds and two English consonant sounds. Most of the major vowel and consonant sounds are covered in the curriculum. Since many pronunciations are influenced by geographic region, you or your students may not agree with some of them! Be aware of this when practicing sounds.

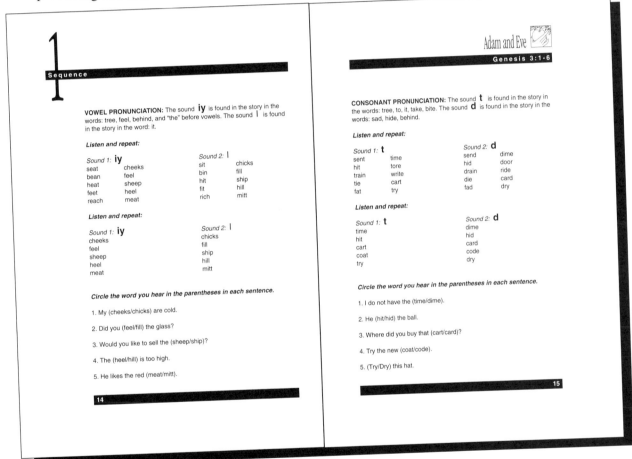

Detailed instructions on teaching the Pronunciation section are given in Chapter 8.

1) Listen and repeat: (about 3–5 minutes)

   a) Do with the whole class and then move on to groups or individuals.

   b) TPR the words that contrast: "Point to <u>cheeks</u>. Touch <u>chick</u>."

2) Circle the word you hear: (5–10 minutes)

This practices distinguishing sounds; you can do this more than once if you like. As students are able, have them give the "test" to each other.

### 1 Sequence

**WORD ORDER:** *Rewrite the sentences correctly.*

| Incorrect | Correct |
|-----------|---------|
| 1. Look at the tree apple. | 1. _____ |
| 2. Throw apple the away. | 2. _____ |
| 3. Grab apple an. | 3. _____ |
| 4. It smell. | 4. _____ |
| 5. The tree to walk. | 5. _____ |

**FILL IN THE BLANKS:** *Fill in the blank with the appropriate word from the following list.*

*apple, You, a, Grab, behind*

1. Hide _____ the tree.
2. _____ feel sad.
3. _____ an apple.
4. Look at the _____ tree.
5. Take _____ bite.

16

## D. WORD ORDER

This is the beginning of the writing exercises. Depending on how you approach them (if you play games), the exercises can take from 15 to 20 minutes to complete and check. I suggest using the written exercises as a "change of pace," perhaps even turning some of them into games. Maybe do a few (rather than all) of the exercises in class and then review them.

1) This exercise reinforces correct word order.

2) Most errors deal with common mistakes such as subjects/nouns, two-word verbs, articles and the location of prepositions (to, at, with, in, of, through).

3) Other activities you can do with this exercise:

   a) Have students read the correct sentences to each other.

   b) Act out the correct sentences for each other.

c) Make cue cards for each word in the sentence. Give the cards to groups of students. Each student takes a card and arranges himself or herself incorrectly first, as in the exercise, then correctly in front of the class to show the sentence.

## E. FILL IN THE BLANK

1) Fill-in-the-blank exercises will help with word order and comprehension.

2) For variety, you can make up additional sentences or have students make up their own from previously learned material.

3) Make a game by competing as teams.

## F. VOCABULARY SUMMARY

1) The summary of lesson vocabulary puts all of the vocabulary from each lesson in three lists: Verbs, Nouns, Other.

a) Each summary details the vocabulary of the lesson.

b) It also serves as a review sheet. (Hold this summary in your hand as you conduct reviews. Use it to generate commands.)

c) Use several summaries at once to help you combine vocabulary of different lessons.

For example:

"Luly, pick up (Sequence #3) the knife (Sequence #2) and take a bite (Sequence #1) of the snake" (Sequence #3).

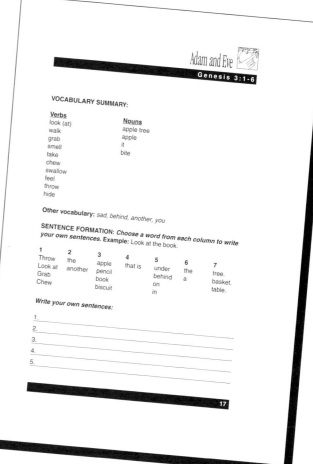

**Adam and Eve**
**Genesis 3:1-6**

VOCABULARY SUMMARY:

**Verbs**
look (at)
walk
grab
smell
take
chew
swallow
feel
throw
hide

**Nouns**
apple tree
apple
it
bite

Other vocabulary: *sad, behind, another, you*

SENTENCE FORMATION: *Choose a word from each column to write your own sentences.* Example: Look at the book.

| 1 | 2 | 3 | 4 | 5 | 6 | 7 |
|---|---|---|---|---|---|---|
| Throw | the | apple | that is | under | the | tree. |
| Look at | another | pencil | | behind | a | basket. |
| Grab | | book | | on | | table. |
| Chew | | biscuit | | in | | |

Write your own sentences:

1. _____
2. _____
3. _____
4. _____
5. _____

17

d) The summary can be used outside of class by an English-speaking friend of the student to direct the student in performing commands.

e) Spelling tests can be given using the key words from the Vocabulary Summary.

## G. SENTENCE FORMATION

1) Explain the example. Give other examples, if necessary. When appropriate, explain tense and person changes that occur in this exercise.

2) Student sentences can be read to the class and acted out when possible.

## H. READING

1) The Bible Passage

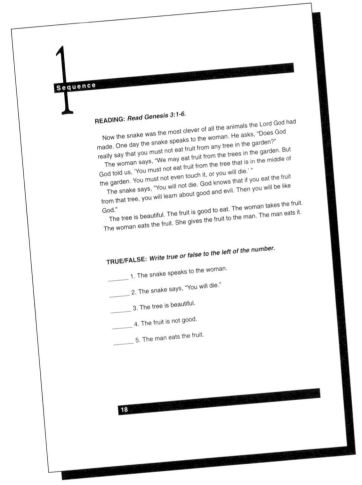

READING: *Read Genesis 3:1-6.*

Now the snake was the most clever of all the animals the Lord God had made. One day the snake speaks to the woman. He asks, "Does God really say that you must not eat fruit from any tree in the garden?"

The woman says, "We may eat fruit from the trees in the garden. But God told us, 'You must not eat fruit from the tree that is in the middle of the garden. You must not even touch it, or you will die.'"

The snake says, "You will not die. God knows that if you eat the fruit from that tree, you will learn about good and evil. Then you will be like God."

The tree is beautiful. The fruit is good to eat. The woman takes the fruit. The woman eats the fruit. She gives the fruit to the man. The man eats it.

TRUE/FALSE: *Write true or false to the left of the number.*

_____ 1. The snake speaks to the woman.

_____ 2. The snake says, "You will die."

_____ 3. The tree is beautiful.

_____ 4. The fruit is not good.

_____ 5. The man eats the fruit.

18

a) The primary purpose of this section is to expose the students directly to Bible passages.

b) In general, only the teacher will be capable of reading the passage. Have students attempt to follow the words with a finger.

Note that, whenever possible, the paraphrased Bible passages have been put into present tense and the language has been simplified.

The reading level is HiBeginner/LowIntermediate. For LowBeginners, difficulty can be reduced with extra practice prior to this exercise and by reading slowly and including gestures.

c) Reading reinforces English word order and intonation patterns. It expands vocabulary and provides listening practice.

d) Capable students can take turns reading.

2) True/False

a) The true-and-false exercises are a non-threatening activity to check comprehension.

b) Do these individually or in groups.

3) Discussion Question. This is not part of the Student Workbook. It is included in each teacher's lesson plan for the Bible Sequences in Chapter 7. Use it as part of each lesson, if at all possible.

a) The purpose of the Discussion Question is to help the students see Christ in the Bible and to learn about having a relationship with Him.

b) The ability of your students to "discuss" a question will vary. With true Beginners, you will not be able to discuss anything in English. However, you can still do several things with this section:

- If nothing else, help students find the answer in the Bible.

- You can go back to the discussion questions at a later date when they are more able to understand.

- Take a few minutes to discuss the question in the students' native language during class, after class or over dinner in your home.

c) If you can't speak the language of your students, invite a guest who does to help you with this part of the lesson.

# How to Teach the Bible Sequences

# Chapter 5

# Teaching a Sequence Step by Step

## A. SETTING UP (1–2 minutes)

1) All Student Workbooks should be closed.

2) Set up the props.

## B. TPR NEW VOCABULARY (10–15 minutes)

1) TPR *some* of the new vocabulary before teaching the Bible Sequence. How much? Leave no more than six to eight new items in a sequence before you teach it. Students will grasp the meaning of some of the new vocabulary as you teach them the sequence.

2) If you are unsure of the students' ability to grasp the new vocabulary, feel free to TPR *all* of the new items before beginning.

## C. MODEL (5–10 minutes)

1) Everyone is observing you.

2) Read and act out each line of the text slowly to ensure full understanding. You will need to have the written text within sight. Do not stop for questions or comments. Act out the sequence several times, expecting a few laughs. Students enjoy watching a teacher perform.

## D. TOGETHER (5 minutes)

1) Say: "Now you are going to do this with me."

2) Distribute the props among the students. If none are available, improvise or mimic.

3) Act out the Bible Sequence together several times. Students only mimic the action. They do not repeat the lines of text. Everyone should be *performing,* not just listening. You will need to keep an eye on the students as they perform to ensure that they are all involved. Phrases such as, "Walk to the tree" can be performed by allowing their "fingers to do the walking" instead of requiring students to leave their seats.

### E. HESITATE (5 minutes)

1) Perform the sequence together, but now **Hesitate** before performing to check student comprehension.

2) Students perform without speaking.

### F. JUMBLE (5 minutes)

1) Give commands from the sequence in random order and observe the students' performance. For example, in Sequence #1 say, "Grab an apple. You feel sad. Walk to the tree." This further checks comprehension.

2) When all are responding well, then proceed.

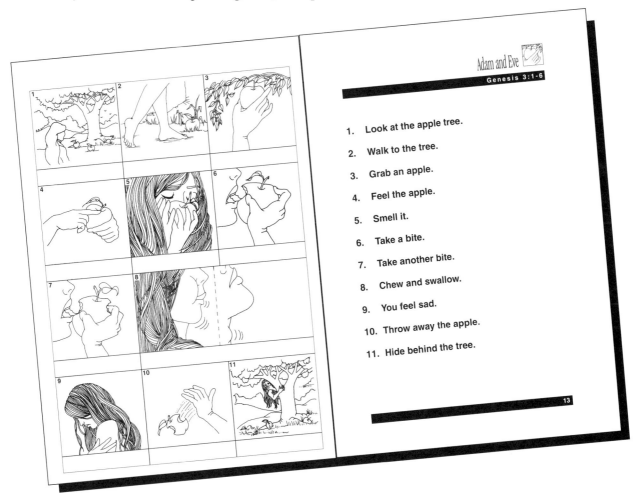

Adam and Eve
**Genesis 3:1-6**

1. Look at the apple tree.

2. Walk to the tree.

3. Grab an apple.

4. Feel the apple.

5. Smell it.

6. Take a bite.

7. Take another bite.

8. Chew and swallow.

9. You feel sad.

10. Throw away the apple.

11. Hide behind the tree.

13

### G. READING AND WRITING (15 minutes)

1) Students now open their books to the sequence pictures.

2) Read the Bible Sequence text to them. As you do, students should attempt to follow the action by pointing to the appropriate picture as they hear each line. At this point, they are listening to the sequence and looking at the pictures.

3) Now students write the Bible Sequence lines below each corresponding picture. For some students, this may seem slow and unnecessary, but it provides several benefits: practice in forming letters, reinforcement of word order and help with spelling. If this slows you down too much, make copies of the picture sequence with the story lines already written below each picture to give to the students.

4) Read the sequence again two or three times as their eyes now follow the written words.

5) TPR the pictures, checking that essential vocabulary is understood. For example, in Sequence #1 you could say, "Touch the tree. Point to the apple. Touch 'Smell it.' Point to 'Feel it.'"

6) Pause here to answer any questions or clarify any subtleties about the language used in the sequence.

### H. SPEAKING (5 minutes)

1) Students repeat each line of the Bible Sequence text after you, using **Backward Build-up** (as a group and with some individuals).

2) In slightly slower-than-normal speech, have the students repeat the sequence after you. Do not speak too quickly!

3) Check for major problems in pronunciation and handle them carefully and with sensitivity.

### I. ROLE REVERSAL (10 minutes)

1) One or more students directs you through the sequence a few times. As you perform, you may want to occasionally make a mistake to check their comprehension.

2) Assign lines to various students. They speak and you perform.

3) One student directs another.

4) Students should now be ready for small-group work.

## J. SMALL-GROUP WORK (15–20 minutes or more)

1) Divide the class into groups of two to four people, with at least one student in each group who is able to repeat the Bible Sequence to the others.

2) In each group, one student repeats the lines of the sequence while the others listen and perform the appropriate action. Only the student who is telling the sequence has his or her book open; other books are closed.

3) As students direct each other through the sequence, they can also use some of the techniques that you have used with them, such as **Hesitate, Jumble** and using TPR with the pictures.

4) Circulate around the room to encourage and help.

*Estimated time to teach a Bible Sequence: 75–90 minutes*

## K. OPTIONS AFTER SMALL-GROUP WORK

1) Groups can perform for each other in front of the class.

2) Expansion activities can be assigned to each group or to the class as a whole.

# Expansion Activities for Conversation Practice

The following activities will help expand the abilities the students have gained through learning the sequences. Many students want to learn "conversational English." These Expansion Activities build toward that goal. The activities can be done with the entire class, in groups or with individuals. The grouping of the activities suggests the appropriate difficulty level. Most of the activities for more advanced students focus on creating conversation.

## FOR ALL STUDENTS

**A. TEACHER ASKS QUESTIONS:** Ask questions about the sequence or individual pictures. Do not ask "why" and "how" questions of Beginners.

1) **Yes/No** questions: "In picture #9, <u>is</u> Eve happy?"

2) **Where** questions: "In picture #1, <u>where</u> is the apple?"

3) **Who** questions: "In picture #4, <u>who</u> has the apple?"

4) "**What** is this?" and "**Is** this___?", asked as teacher points to an object in the pictures.

5) **Can** questions: "In picture #4, <u>can</u> Eve feel the apple?"

**B. STUDENTS ASK QUESTIONS:** Students ask similar questions about the sequence or individual pictures, talking to the teacher or other students.

**C. SUBSTITUTION DRILLS:** The teacher gives the pattern sentence and a cue vocabulary word. Students repeat the pattern sentence using the cue vocabulary word.

For example:   Teacher: "Apple. Grab the apple."
                    Teacher: "Book."
                    Student: "Grab the **book.**"

Or:             Teacher: "Feel. Feel the apple."
                    Teacher: "Smell."
                    Student: "**Smell** the apple."

**D. QUESTION-CHAIN DRILL:** The teacher begins by asking a question. A student answers the question, then that student asks the same question of another student.

For example:   Teacher: "Where is the book?"
                    Student 1: "It's on the table."
                    Student 1: "Where is the book?"
                    Student 2: "It's on the table."

Also:          Teacher: "Where is the book?"
                    Student 1: "It's on the table."
                    Student 1: "Where is the pencil?"
                    Student 2: "It's under the book."

**E. JUMBLE AND MATCH PICTURES:**
1) Photocopy the pictures and the text. Cut out the sequence pictures; block out the numbers. Cut out the sentences. Scramble the pictures. Students put them in the correct order.

2) Give students a scrambled pile of pictures and a scrambled list of sequence sentences. Have students match the picture with the appropriate sentence.

3) Give students a pile of pictures with no text. Students write the correct text below each picture and then arrange the pictures in the correct order.

**F. TEACHER DESCRIBES A PICTURE:** The teacher describes in detail a picture from the sequence. Some suggestions: Refer to the action, clothing, body position, background and other details. Students guess which picture is being described.

**G. DELIBERATE MISTAKES:** The teacher tells the story having warned students that deliberate mistakes will be made. Students indicate the errors made and the corrections needed.

For example: Sequence #1, line 3,    Teacher: "Grab a book."
Student: "Not book, apple."

**H. PAUSE IN THE STORYLINE:** The teacher recites the sequence, pausing occasionally for students to complete the sentences.

For example: Sequence #1, line 2,    Teacher: "Walk to the ____."
Student: "Tree."

**I. STUDENTS CREATE THEIR OWN SEQUENCES:** The teacher supplies groups of students with vocabulary and has each group create a simple sequence. Students then perform the new sequence.

## FOR MORE ADVANCED STUDENTS

**A. TEACHER ASKS QUESTIONS:** The teacher asks "what," "why" and "how" questions about the sequence or individual pictures. The questions may be formed in different tenses. When an answer is not found in the story, students need to make up their own answers.

For example:    1) **What:** "In Sequence #1, picture #3, <u>what</u> is Eve doing?"

"In Sequence #1, picture #3, <u>what</u> did Eve do?

2) **Why:** "In Sequence #1, picture #3, <u>why</u> does Eve grab the apple?"

3) **How:** "In Sequence #1, picture #3, <u>how</u> does Eve grab the apple?"

**B. STUDENTS ASK QUESTIONS:** Students ask similar questions about the sequence or individual pictures to the teacher or other students.

**C. CHANGE TENSES:** Students change a sequence orally or in writing from present tense to present continuous or simple past. Give students the past-tense spelling and pronunciation of verbs. (See page 85 for a full discussion.)

**D. STUDENTS DESCRIBE PICTURES:** Students describe, as they are able, a specific picture. They can refer to the action, clothing, body position, background and other details. The other students guess which frame is being described.

**E. TRANSFORMATION DRILLS:** The teacher gives a pattern sentence. Students respond with the transformation desired.

For example:
1) **Positive to negative/negative to positive**
Teacher: "She has the book."
Student: "She doesn't have the book."

2) **Statement to a question/question to a statement**
Teacher: "There is an apple in the tree."
Student: "Is there an apple in the tree?"

3) **From one tense to another**
Teacher: "She grabs the apple."
Student: "She grabbed the apple."

4) **From plural to singular/singular to plural**
Teacher: "I grab the apple."
Student: "We grab the apple."

5) **From a personal noun to a pronoun**
Teacher: "Eve grabs the apple."
Student: "She grabs the apple."

**F. EMBELLISH THE STORY:** The teacher retells the Bible Sequence, adding details. The teacher pauses after each picture, to either ask questions or respond to student questions. Roles can be reversed, with students embellishing the original story.

For example:   Sequence #1, picture #1

Teacher:   "One afternoon Eve is walking in the garden. She feels tired and hungry. She sees an apple tree. She likes apples."

Teacher:   "Does Eve like apples?"

Or:

Student:   "How old is Eve?"

**G. LISTEN AND SUMMARIZE:** After students listen to a portion of an embellished story, they summarize the story for other students.

**H. RETELL A SEQUENCE:** Students are given a copy of the sequence pictures with no text. Using the picture page only as a reference, they retell the story.

**I. STUDENTS INVENT A VARIATION OF THE ORIGINAL STORY:** Give the students a cue that changes the story. They invent a variation.

For example:   Sequence #6, picture #5
Teacher:   "Knock on the door. Oops! Wrong house!"
Student:   "_____." (Invents a response.)

**J. RETELL ABBREVIATED STORIES:** The teacher tells short stories based on pictures in the sequence. Students retell the story as they hear it. Stories should be from two to five sentences long. (This may appear easy to you, but it is not for them!) For example:

Teacher:   "Eve is alone. She is walking in the garden. She grabs an apple."

Student:   "_____."(Tries to retell the same story in his/her own words. )

**K. STUDENTS WRITE THEIR OWN STORIES:** Students write their own brief stories, using the sequence as a reference.

# Teaching Tense Changes

The major thrust of the Student Workbook is the **present tense.** Other tenses are included in the 15 Bible Sequences (see below) and in the Sentence Formation exercises, but most of the written exercises are in the present tense. Changing tenses is an **optional activity** included in the Expansion Activities (Chapter 5). For changing tenses, the following information will be helpful.

First, a word of caution. What you *could* attempt to do in this area and what you *should* attempt may be two different things. The success of the students should determine how much you try to accomplish. Stay with one tense until they consistently have success. If you cover only one or two tenses by the end of the course, that is fine. For students who want more work with tenses, you could go back through the sequences and written exercises again, working on new tenses.

I usually wait until students have had 25 to 30 hours of TPR before introducing a tense change. Until that time, they are focused on the present tense only. Even after a new tense is introduced, the present tense is still continually practiced.

The eight Beginning Lessons should take about two hours each. The Bible Sequence chapters take about four hours each if you include adequate TPR work, time to learn the sequence and time to do the exercises and some Expansion Activities. The first tense change should be introduced then about the time you reach Sequence #5, "Jonah Is Angry." (Jonah introduces the present continuous, "You are sitting in the house.") Sequence #4, "David and Goliath," introduces "You're going to," but I suggest you begin with the present continuous. It works well with TPR.

## A. INTRODUCING THE PRESENT CONTINUOUS

$$I + am + verb + ing$$

By the time the students reach "Jonah Is Angry," they have internalized dozens of verbs. They will now learn to add "I + am" + "verb + ing" to verbs they already know. Let's drop in on our teacher from Chapter 1 as she introduces the present continuous in her TPR classroom.

She begins by **Modeling** two verbs. She points to the door. As she does so, she asks herself, "Teacher, what are you doing?" She answers slowly, "I am pointing to the door." (She repeats.) Then she touches the table. As she does so she asks herself, "Teacher, what are you doing?" She answers slowly, "I am touching the table." She **Models** this a few times.

Now she writes on the board, "What are you doing?" She repeats the question a few times and then does **Backward Build-up** to help the students produce the question. She emphasizes the "ing" sound because it is new.

The students write the question down. She proceeds to **Model** again the answers, "I am pointing to the door. I am touching the table." She then writes the sentences on the board. She underlines "I," "am," "point," "ing," "touch," "ing." She then explains how the present continuous is formed: I + am + verb + ing.

On the board, she writes "smell," another verb they know. She smells a book and says, "I am smelling the book." They each pick up a book and as they smell it each one says, "I am smelling the book."

She writes on the board "picking up." She **Models** and says, "I am picking up the book." The students follow her lead. They practice these sentences several times together. They now write in their books each of the commands they have practiced thus far.

The teacher decides to skip the **Together** technique and goes into the **Alone** technique. She calls on Raul. She says, "Point to the book." Raul performs. She asks, "What are you doing?" He responds, "I am point to the book." The teacher **Models** the correct response and Raul repeats. She says, "Touch the door." He performs. She asks, "Raul, what are you doing?" He responds slowly, "I am touching the door." She continues to call on various students using the **Alone** technique and familiar verbs.

After they have developed some confidence, she calls on students who can do **Role Reversal.** They now take her place in giving commands and asking questions. She allows the students to work on their own but is there to **Model** answers whenever help is needed.

Now that she has introduced the present continuous, she can use it at any time in the future as part of her review. The next time in class, she may list several familiar verbs on the board and ask the students how to change them to the present continuous. They will then practice performing the verbs in present continuous. She can also use **Cue Cards** or practice the Sentence Formation exercise to change sentences to the present continuous.

## B. THE PATTERN THE TEACHER USES

*The following pattern may be followed to introduce other new tenses.*

1) **Model** the action, the question and the answer.

2) Write the question and the answer on the board.

3) Explain briefly what is happening to the language.

4) Practice **Backward Build-up** to pronounce the sentences. Emphasize the new sounds, especially the sounds that form the past tense in English. They are particularly hard for students to hear and reproduce. For help with teaching the past tense, see Chapter 8, Section F, "How to Pronounce the Past Tense."

5) Students write down the sentences.

6) Teacher and students perform commands **Together** using the new tense.

7) Students perform **Alone.**

8) Students do **Role Reversal.**

9) The new tense is incorporated into future review.

## C. COMBINING TENSES

If you have the students long enough or if you begin with more advanced speakers, you can combine several tenses in TPR practice.

For example:  Teacher:  "Carlos, what are you going to do?"
Carlos:  "I am going to point to the door."
Teacher:  "Carlos, point to the door!"

Carlos performs.

Teacher:  "Carlos, what are you doing?"
Carlos:  "I am pointing to the door."
Teacher:  "Carlos, what did you do?"
Carlos:  "I pointed to the door.

## D. CHANGING PERSONS

For more advanced students, you can begin to practice the tenses with different persons (first, second, third, singular and plural). The picture sequence pages are a helpful aid in doing this.

For example, in Sequence #2, frame #3: "What is Abraham doing?" "He is cutting wood."

In frame #1: "What are Abraham and his son doing?" "They are going to the mountain."

In frame #8: "What did Abraham do?" "He tied up his son."

## E. TENSES FOUND IN THE BIBLE SEQUENCES

1) **Present tense only**
   Sequence #s 1, 2, 3, 9

2) **Present continuous**
   Sequence  #5: "You are sitting in the house."
   #10: "Where is the seed growing?"
   #13: "You're walking down the road."
   #14: "You are coming in from the fields."
   #15: "You are running quickly to the tomb of Jesus."

3) **Future using "going to" or "will"**
   Sequence  #4: "You're going to fight Goliath."
   #6: "You're going to see the baby Jesus."
   #7: "You're going to get some wine."
   #8: "You're going to see Jesus today."
   #10: "You're going to plant some seed."
   #13: "I will return tomorrow."

4) **Simple past**
   Sequence  #8: "What a day it was!"
   #11: "You found it. I found my lost coin."

5) **Present perfect**
   Sequence  #7: "The water has changed into wine."
   #15: "He is risen."

# Beginning Lessons

# Chapter 6

# Introduction to Beginning Lessons

**A. WHERE SHOULD THE TEACHER BEGIN?** For *True* and *False Beginners,* start at Lesson 1. For *HiBeginners,* try starting at the first review lesson, Lesson 4. If the students are not mostly successful, then return to Lesson 1 or 2; if they do well with Lesson 4, then move on to Lesson 5.

If your students are *LowIntermediates,* plan on doing Lesson 4 and Lesson 8 to find out how much vocabulary is unfamiliar to them. If necessary, put together a TPR lesson specifically for the vocabulary they do not understand. If they do well with Lessons 4 and 8, then move on to the Bible Sequences.

Also keep in mind that with *LowIntermediates,* you can switch more quickly to **Role Reversal** and should expect the students to participate orally right from the beginning.

**B. SHOULD YOU DO ALL EIGHT TPR LESSONS BEFORE START-ING THE BIBLE SEQUENCES?** Not necessarily. If you meet for only one (1) hour a week, for example, it would take you nearly 16 weeks to reach the Bible Sequences. You could begin the sequences after Lesson 4 and return to the beginning TPR lessons after doing Bible Sequence 2 or 3.

**C. WHAT ABOUT COLORS, BODY PARTS AND SURVIVAL TEXTS?** One color is suggested for each of Lessons 1 to 3 and 5 to 7 in the following Beginning Lesson Plans. Try to find props with the suggested color, or simply teach a color with props you already have available. Body parts are fun to teach using TPR ("Touch your nose." "Point to your arm."). Include body parts in the lessons if you wish. Survival texts are also provided to you as optional material. Include them at your discretion when the students are comfortable speaking in class.

Continue to work on these items and others (days of the week, telling time and so on) even after having begun the 15 Bible Sequences. These practical items are helpful to the students and provide a change of pace from the sequences.

**D. THE "BIG" LITTLE WORDS.** Often in learning another language, the "little" words, such as prepositions, are difficult to master. You will note an early emphasis in the TPR lessons on such words as: in, on, under, with, up, down and so on. Clearly distinguishing these words through TPR work will greatly help students internalize this part of the language.

# Beginning Lesson #1

**Verbs:** stand (up), sit (down), walk, (don't) stop, turn (around), touch, point (to)

**Vocabulary:** slowly, quickly, again, the, and, table, chair, book, paper, pencil

**Props:** table, chair, book, blue book, pencil, paper, blue paper

## A. WELCOME AND INTRODUCTION TO THE COURSE (10 minutes)

If you cannot speak the students' language, have someone help you, or simply begin.

## B. BEGIN TPR (15 minutes)

Begin with two to three volunteers. Then include others. Work with each new item until students are successful. Then move on.

1) Verbs: **stand up/sit down (Modeling)**

2) Verbs: **walk, stop, turn around (Modeling)**

3) Vocabulary: **slowly** (Use with previous verbs.)

> For example:  "Stand up slowly. Sit down slowly."
> "Stand up slowly. Walk slowly. Stop. Turn around slowly."
> "Walk slowly. Stop. Turn around. Sit down slowly."

Continue practice, using **Chain Commands** with a variety of students.
**Hesitate** occasionally to check comprehension.
Direct students using the **Alone** technique. If they fail, **Model** for them.

> USE:
> **Model**
> **Together**
> **Hesitate**
> **Alone**

## C. NUMBERS (10 minutes) (Refer to Chapter 2.)

## D. NEW TPR (15 minutes)

1) Vocabulary: **quickly** (Use with previous verbs.)

2) When students are comfortable with "quickly," combine it with "slowly."

   For example:  "Stand up slowly. Walk quickly. Stop."
   "Turn around quickly. Walk slowly. Stop."
   "Turn around slowly. Sit down quickly."

3) Verb: **touch** (Introduce along with table, chair and book.)

   For example:  "Walk. Stop. Touch the table."
   "Turn around slowly. Touch the book."
   "Walk quickly. Stop. Touch the chair."
   "Walk slowly to the table. Touch the book."

Continue to work with these four new items using **Model, Together, Hesitate** and **Alone.** After students are successful, move on.

4) Vocabulary: **blue** (Use with book.)

## E. BREAK (10 minutes)

## F. ALPHABET (10 minutes) (Refer to Chapter 2.)

## G. NEW TPR (15–20 minutes)

1) Verb: **point to** (Use with table, chair, book.)

   For example: "Walk to the table. Touch the book. Point to the book."

2) Vocabulary: **paper, pencil** (Use with touch and point to.)

3) Vocabulary: **again** (Use with previous verbs.)

   For example: "Stand up. Walk to the table and touch the book. Touch the book again. Walk quickly to the chair. Sit down slowly. Stand up again."

4) Vocabulary: **don't** (Use with all previous verbs.)

For example: "Stand up slowly. Walk. Don't stop. Stop! Touch the book. Don't touch the pencil, touch the paper. Turn around slowly. Walk quickly. Stop. Don't sit down quickly. Sit down slowly."

## H. REVIEW ALL TPR WORK (10 minutes)

Using **Chain Commands** and the **Connective** "and," review all the vocabulary.

Try to be spontaneous. Let the commands "flow." They do not need to be given in any special order. If students fail, you may be going too fast and giving them too much at once. When they fail, **Model** for them!

> **USE:**
> **Model**
> **Together**
> **Hesitate**
> **Alone**

## I. DO VOCABULARY SUMMARY/ADDITIONAL ITEMS/SENTENCE FORMATION (Student Workbook) (15 minutes)

1) Pronounce each vocabulary word and perform the action as students listen. (This now connects the eyes to words.)

2) Demonstrate clearly how the sentences are formed. Then do it together, individually or for homework. Read some of the students' sentences and perform the action.

# Beginning Lesson #2

**Verbs:** jump, pick (up), put (down, on, in, under), take (out)

**Vocabulary:** box, bag, basket, tree, knife, wood, rope, snake, apple, big, little

**Props:** box, bag, basket, tree, wood, rope, snake, apple, knife, red prop

USE:
Model
Together
Hesitate
Alone

## A. REVIEW TPR WORK FROM LESSON 1 (15 minutes)
(Remember to include numbers, alphabet and colors in review.)

## B. NEW NUMBERS (10 minutes)

USE:
Model
Together
Hesitate
Alone

## C. NEW TPR (15–20 minutes)
Work with each new item until students are successful, then move on.

1) Vocabulary: **basket, box** (Use with touch, point to, and don't.)

2) Verbs: **pick up, put down** (Introduce together with previous objects.)

3) Vocabulary: **bag, apple** (Use with touch, point to, and pick up.)

4) Do a "mini-review" before break.

## D. BREAK (10 minutes)

## E. NEW ALPHABET (10 minutes)

**F. NEW TPR (15–20 minutes)**

USE:
Model
Together
Hesitate
Alone

1) Vocabulary: **tree, knife, snake** (Use with touch, point to, pick up, put down.)

2) Verb: **put under** (Use with previous objects.)

    For example: "Pick up the snake. Put the snake under the box."

3) Vocabulary: **rope, wood, red** (Use with previous verbs.)

    For example: "Walk slowly to the table and pick up the rope."

4) Verbs: **put in, take out** (Introduce together with box, bag, basket.)

5) Verb: **jump** (Introduce with previous verbs.)

6) Verb: **put on** (Introduce in contrast with put under and put in.)

For example:   "Put the apple on the box. Put the snake in the bag."
                    "Don't put the apple in the box. Put the apple on the box."

**G. QUESTION: "WHAT IS THIS?" "THAT?" (10 minutes) (Refer to Chapter 2, "Teaching Questions.")**

**H. REVIEW ALL NEW TPR WORK (10 minutes)**

USE:
Model
Together
Hesitate
Alone

**I. DO VOCABULARY SUMMARY/ADDITIONAL ITEMS/SENTENCE FORMATION (Student Workbook) (15 minutes)**

1) Pronounce each vocabulary word and perform the action as students listen. (This now connects the eyes to words.)

2) Demonstrate clearly how the sentences are formed. Then do it together, individually or for homework. Read some of the students' sentences and perform the action.

# Beginning Lesson #3

**Verbs:** grab, go/come (to), hide, look (at), carry

**Vocabulary:** one, stick, stone, sling, both, house, sandals, hand(s), one, both

**Props**: stick, stone, sling, house, sandals, green prop

**USE:**
**Model**
**Together**
**Hesitate**
**Alone**

## A. REVIEW TPR WORK FROM LESSONS 1 & 2 (15 minutes)

(Do not begin Lesson #3 until students are successful.)

## B. NEW ALPHABET (10 minutes) (Refer to Chapter 2.)

## C. NEW TPR (15–20 minutes)

**USE:**
**Model**
**Together**
**Hesitate**
**Alone**

1) Vocabulary: **stick, stone** (Use with touch, point, pick up, put, etc.)

2) Verb: **grab** (Use with previous objects.)

   For example: "Grab the stone and the stick."

3) Vocabulary: **house, sling** (Use with previous verbs.)

4) Verb: **hide** (Use with previous objects and position word such as: in, under, on.)

## D. BREAK (10 minutes)

**E. NEW NUMBERS (10 minutes) (Refer to Chapter 2.)**

**F. NEW TPR (15–20 minutes)**
1) Vocabulary: **sandal, green** (Use with previous verbs.)

2) Verb: **look at** (Use with previous objects.)

3) Verb: **carry** (Use with previous objects.)

4) Verb: **go to / come to** (Introduce together.)

    For example:    "Go to the table. Touch the book. Come to the chair."
                    "Come to the table. Go to the house."

5) Vocabulary:   **one / both / hand**(s) (Introduce together.)
                     (Use with previous objects.)

    For example:    "Pick up one book. Pick up both pencils. Pick up the pencil
                    with one hand. Pick up the book with both hands."

> USE:
> Model
> Together
> Hesitate
> Alone

**G. QUESTION: "IS THIS _____?" "YES, IT IS. / NO, IT ISN'T."
(10 minutes)**

**H. REVIEW ALL NEW TPR WORK (10 minutes)**

> USE:
> Model
> Together
> Hesitate
> Alone

**I. DO VOCABULARY SUMMARY/ADDITIONAL ITEMS/SENTENCE
FORMATION (Student Workbook) (15 minutes)**
1) Pronounce each vocabulary word and perform the action as students
listen. (This now connects the eyes to words.)

2) Demonstrate clearly how the sentences are formed. Then do it together,
individually or for homework. Read some of the students' sentences and
perform the action.

# Beginning Lesson #4 (Review of #s 1, 2 & 3)

**Introduction:** Fill in the outline below as needed to help you conduct the lesson. Generate commands, working with groups of two to three verbs at a time. First review by lesson, then try mixing the vocabulary from the different lessons.

For example: "Go to the table. Pick up the apple and hide the apple in the box."

Also, review all the numbers, letters, colors and any other material you have covered.

**Verbs:** stand (up), sit (down), walk, (don't) stop, turn (around), touch, point (to), jump, pick (up), put (down, in, on, under), take (out), grab, go/come (to), hide, look (at), carry

**Vocabulary:** up, down, in, on, under, out, slowly, quickly, knife, big, table, little, stone, sling, house, wood, hands, again, the chair (book, paper, pencil), and, stick, box, bag, basket, rope, snake, apple, sandals

## A) TPR REVIEW OF LESSONS 1 & 2 (15–20 minutes)

USE:
Model
Together
Hesitate
Alone

## B) NUMBERS REVIEW (10–15 minutes)

## C) QUESTION REVIEW: "WHAT IS THIS?" "WHAT IS THAT?" (5 minutes)

**D) TPR REVIEW LESSON 3 (10–15 minutes)**

**E) BREAK (10 minutes)**

**F) ALPHABET REVIEW (10–15 minutes)**

**G) QUESTION REVIEW: "IS THIS _____?" "YES, IT IS. / NO, IT ISN'T."
(5 minutes)**

**H) TPR REVIEW: COMBINING LESSONS 1, 2 & 3 (10–15 minutes)**

**I) DO VOCABULARY SUMMARY/ADDITIONAL ITEMS/SENTENCE FORMATION (Student Workbook) (15 minutes)**

1) Pronounce each vocabulary word and perform the action as students listen. (This now connects the eyes to words.)

2) Demonstrate clearly how the sentences are formed. Then do it together, individually or for homework. Read some of the students' sentences and perform the action.

# Beginning Lesson #5

**Verbs:** feel, smell, rub, cut, cover, hold

**Vocabulary:** orange (the fruit), bush, altar, face, seed, sad, happy, hole, that is

**Props:** orange, bush, altar, seed, hole

## A. REVIEW TPR FROM LESSON 4 (15 minutes)

USE:
Model
Together
Hesitate
Alone

## B. NEW NUMBERS (10 minutes) (Refer to Chapter 2.)

## C. NEW TPR (15–20 minutes)

1) Verb: **feel** (Introduce with previous vocabulary.)

   For example: "Feel the apple. Point to the book. Feel the book."

2) Verb: **smell** (Introduce with previous vocabulary.)

   For example: "Don't feel the apple. Smell the apple."

3) Vocabulary: **orange, bush, seed** (Introduce with feel, smell, look at, etc.)

4) Verb: **rub** (Introduce with previous vocabulary.)

5) Vocabulary: **altar, hole** (Introduce with previous vocabulary.)

USE:
Model
Together
Hesitate
Alone

## D. BREAK (10 minutes)

## E. NEW ALPHABET (10 minutes)

## F. NEW TPR (15–20 minutes)

1) Vocabulary: **that is** (Introduce with previous vocabulary.)

   For example: "Feel the orange that is on the table."

2) Verb: **cover** (Introduce with previous vocabulary.)

   For example: "Cover the pencil with one hand."

3) Vocabulary: **face, happy, sad** (Introduce face with previous vocabulary; use facial expressions, drawings, etc., to communicate happy/sad.)

4) Verb: **hold** (Introduce with previous vocabulary.)

   For example: "Hold the orange and sit down."

5) Verb: **cut** (Introduce with orange, paper, bag, wood, apple, etc.)

> USE:
> Model
> Together
> Hesitate
> Alone

## G. QUESTION: "CAN YOU _____?" "YES, I CAN. / NO, I CAN'T." (10 minutes) (Refer to Chapter 2, "Teaching Questions.")

## H. DO VOCABULARY SUMMARY/ADDITIONAL ITEMS/SENTENCE FORMATION (Student Workbook) (15 minutes)

1) Pronounce each vocabulary word and perform the action as students listen. (This now connects the eyes to words.)

2) Demonstrate clearly how the sentences are formed. Then do it together, individually or for homework. Read some of the students' sentences and perform the action.

# Beginning Lesson #6

**Verbs:** bend (down), run, follow, give, give (back)

**Vocabulary:** star, can (pitcher), fish, towel, gift, coins, his, her, your

**Props:** star, can, fish, towel, gift (box), coins

## A. TPR REVIEW OF LESSON 5 (15 minutes)

USE:
Model
Together
Hesitate
Alone

## B. NEW NUMBERS (10 minutes) (Refer to Chapter 2.)

## C. NEW TPR (15–20 minutes)

1) Verb: **bend down** (slowly, quickly, again, etc.)

   For example: "Walk to the table and bend down slowly."

2) Verb: **run** (If necessary, let students' fingers "do the running.")

   For example: "Run to the table and feel the apple."

3) Vocabulary: **towel, star, coins** (touch, point to, rub, smell, etc.)

4) Verb: **give to** (Introduce with previous objects.)

5) Verb: **give back** (**Recombine** with **give.**)

USE:
Model
Together
Hesitate
Alone

## D. BREAK (10 minutes)

**E. NEW ALPHABET (10 minutes)**

**F. NEW TPR (15–20 minutes)**

1) Verb: **follow** (Use with people moving, lines on the floor, board, wall, etc.)

   For example: "(Student #1), go to the table. (Student #2) follow (Student #1) to the table."

2) Vocabulary: **his** (Introduce with familiar vocabulary.)

   For example: "Pick up his book."

3) Vocabulary: **her** (Introduce with familiar vocabulary.)

4) Vocabulary: **your** (Introduce with familiar vocabulary.)

5) Vocabulary: **can** (pitcher), **fish, gift** (Introduce with familiar verbs.)

**USE:**
Model
Together
Hesitate
Alone

**G. QUESTION: "WHERE IS _____?" "IT'S _____." (10 minutes) (Refer to Chapter 2, "Teaching Questions.")**

**H. TPR REVIEW OF DAY'S VOCABULARY (10 minutes)**

**USE:**
Model
Together
Hesitate
Alone

**I. DO VOCABULARY SUMMARY/ADDITIONAL ITEMS/SENTENCE FORMATION (Student Workbook) (15 minutes)**

1) Pronounce each vocabulary word and perform the action as students listen. (This now connects the eyes to words.)

2) Demonstrate clearly how the sentences are formed. Then do it together, individually or for homework. Read some of the students' sentences and perform the action.

# Beginning Lesson #7

**Verbs:** have/has, get, pour, fill (up), wrap, dry

**Vocabulary:** pitcher, a glass, oil, water, wine, cloth, some, several

**Props:** 3 pitchers (one labeled "water," another labeled "wine" and another labeled "oil"), a drinking glass, a piece of cloth

**USE:**
Model
Together
Hesitate
Alone

## A. TPR REVIEW OF LESSON 6 (15 minutes)

## B. NEW NUMBERS AND ALPHABET (15–20 minutes)

**USE:**
Model
Together
Hesitate
Alone

## C. NEW TPR (15–20 minutes)

1) Verb: **have** (Introduce with familiar vocabulary.)

For example: "I have a towel."
"I don't have the towel. I have the coin."

2) Verb: **has** (Introduce with familiar vocabulary.)

3) Vocabulary: **pitcher, a glass, cloth** (Introduce one at a time.)

## D. QUESTION: "WHO HAS _____?" (10 minutes) (Refer to Chapter 2.)

## E. BREAK (10 minutes)

## F. NEW TPR (15–20 minutes)

USE:
Model
Together
Hesitate
Alone

1) Verb: **get** (Introduce with familiar vocabulary.)

2) Vocabulary: **water, wine, oil** (Introduce with familiar vocabulary.)

3) Verbs: **pour, fill (up)** (Introduce together with familiar vocabulary.)

   Example: "Pour water in the glass. Fill the glass up."

4) Vocabulary: **some, several** (Introduce together.)

   **count nouns:** books, pencils, apples, etc.
   **non-count nouns:** water, oil, wine, rice, etc.

   "Some" can be used with count and non-count nouns.
   "Several" cannot be used with non-count nouns.

   Examples: "I have some books."     (right)
       "I have some water."     (right)

       "I have several books."   (right)
       "I have several water."   (wrong)

5) Verbs: **wrap, dry** (Introduce with familiar vocabulary.)

## G. REVIEW QUESTIONS FROM LESSONS 2–6 (5 minutes)

## H. DO VOCABULARY SUMMARY/ADDITIONAL ITEMS/SENTENCE FORMATION (Student Workbook) (15 minutes)

1) Pronounce each vocabulary word and perform the action as students listen. (This now connects the eyes to words.)

2) Demonstrate clearly how the sentences are formed. Then do it together, individually or for homework. Read some of the students' sentences and perform the action.

# Beginning Lesson #8 (Review of #s 5, 6 & 7)

**Introduction:** Fill in the outline below as needed to help you conduct the lesson. Generate commands, working with groups of two to three verbs at a time. First review by lesson, then try mixing the vocabulary from the different lessons.

Also review all the numbers, letters, colors and any other material you have covered.

**Verbs:** feel, smell, rub, cut, cover, hold, hit, (don't) dry, bend (down), run, follow, give, give (back), leave, have/has, get, pour, fill (up), wrap

**Vocabulary:** orange, bush, altar, face, oil, seed, star, cloth, fish, towel, gift, pitcher, a glass, water, wine, sad, happy, hole, that is, can (pitcher), coins, his, her, your, several, some, down, back

## A. TPR REVIEW OF LESSONS 5 & 6 (15–20 minutes)

USE:
Model
Together
Hesitate
Alone

## B. NUMBERS REVIEW: (10–15 minutes)

## C. QUESTION REVIEW: "CAN YOU _____?" "YES, I CAN. / NO, I CAN'T." (5 minutes)

**D. TPR REVIEW OF LESSON 7 (10–15 minutes)**

USE:
Model
Together
Hesitate
Alone

**E. BREAK (10 minutes)**

**F. ALPHABET REVIEW (10–15 minutes)**

**G. QUESTION REVIEW: "WHERE IS _____?" "IT'S _____."**
**(5 minutes)**

**H. TPR REVIEW COMBINING LESSONS 5, 6 & 7 (10–15 minutes)**

USE:
Model
Together
Hesitate
Alone

**I. DO VOCABULARY SUMMARY/ADDITIONAL ITEMS/SENTENCE**
**FORMATION (Student Workbook) (15 minutes)**

1) Pronounce each vocabulary word and perform the action as students listen. (This now connects the eyes to words.)

2) Demonstrate clearly how the sentences are formed. Then do it together, individually or for homework. Read some of the students' sentences and perform the action.

# Lesson Plans for Each Bible Sequence

**7**

Sequence #1: Adam and Eve (Genesis 3:1–6)

**REVIEW WITH STUDENTS:** Choose some of the following items for review before beginning this sequence: vocabulary, questions, alphabet, numbers, colors, survival texts (optional), previous sequences, expansion activities.

**TAKE NOTE:** Clearly demonstrate the difference between "feel" (line 4) and "feel" (line 9). Show that "it" refers to apple (line 5). "Bite" is a noun (lines 6 and 7).

1. Look at the apple tree.
2. Walk to the tree.
3. Grab an apple.
4. Feel the apple.
5. Smell it.
6. Take a bite.
7. Take another bite.
8. Chew and swallow.
9. You feel sad.
10. Throw away the apple.
11. Hide behind the tree.

## *TEACHING THE SEQUENCE STEP BY STEP*

### A. SET UP THE PROPS (1–2 minutes)

### B. TPR NEW VOCABULARY (10–15 minutes)
**Verbs:** chew, swallow, throw away
**Vocabulary:** it, behind, tree, another, bite, you

### C. MODEL (5 minutes)
1) Everyone is observing you.
2) Read and act out the Bible Sequence several times.

### D. TOGETHER (5 minutes)
1) "Now you are going to do this with me."

### E. HESITATE (5 minutes)
1) Say each line, but you hesitate before performing.

### F. JUMBLE (5 minutes)
1) Give commands from the text in random order.

### G. READING AND WRITING (15 minutes)
1) Students now open their books to the sequence pictures.
2) Read Sequence #1 to them. They follow the pictures.
3) Students write the sequence lines below each picture.
4) Read the sequence two or three times. Students follow the written words.
5) TPR the pictures.
6) Pause for questions and to point out language subtleties.

### H. SPEAKING (10 minutes)
1) Do **Backward Build-up** for each line of the sequence.
2) Repeat the Bible Sequence in normal speech. Speak slowly.
3) Listen for major pronunciation problems.

### I. ROLE REVERSAL (10 minutes)
1) One or more students direct you through the sequence.
2) Assign sequence lines to students.
3) One student directs another.

### J. SMALL-GROUP WORK (15–20 minutes)
1) Students direct each other. Books are closed, except for the speaker's.
2) Combine these techniques: **Hesitate, Jumble** and TPR the pictures.
3) Circulate around the room to encourage and help.

### EXPANSION ACTIVITIES: (Refer to Chapter 5.)

Recommended for early sequences:
- Questions from Beginning Lessons:
  What is this? Is this_____? Where is _____? Who has _____?
- Substitution drills
- Question-chain drills
- Jumble and match pictures
- Deliberate mistakes

### PRONUNCIATION:

Follow the suggestions given in Chapter 8. Focus on the sounds, not on teaching the vocabulary in this section.

### WORD ORDER:

Follow suggestions given for this exercise on page 70.

Answers:

1) Look at the apple tree.
2) Throw away the apple.
3) Grab an apple.
4) Smell it.
5) Walk to the tree.

### FILL IN THE BLANK:

Follow suggestions given for this exercise on page 70.

Answers:

1) behind
2) You
3) Grab
4) apple
5) a

## VOCABULARY SUMMARY:

| Verbs | Nouns |
|-------|-------|
| look (at) | tree |
| walk | apple |
| grab | it |
| smell | bite |
| take | |
| chew | |
| swallow | |
| feel | |
| throw | |
| hide | |

**Other vocabulary:** sad, behind, another, you

## SENTENCE FORMATION:

Explain the example. Give other examples, if necessary. When appropriate, explain tense and person changes that occur in this exercise.

## READING:

1) True/False: 1-T, 2-F, 3-T, 4-F, 5-T.

2) Discussion section: As a result of disobedience, sin enters the world. Immediately after this incident, the Lord draws the battle line between Himself and the Devil (Genesis 3:15).

   a) Read Genesis 3:15 together: "I will make you (the devil) and the woman enemies to each other. Your descendants and her descendants will be enemies. Her child will crush your head. And you will bite his heel."

   b) Question for students: Who is "Her child"?

   c) Additional verses: Galatians 4:4; 1 John 3:8; Colossians 2:15; Hebrews 2:14.

## Sequence #2: Abraham and His Son (Genesis 22:1–12)

**REVIEW WITH STUDENTS:** Choose some of the following items for review before beginning this sequence: vocabulary, questions, alphabet, numbers, colors, survival texts (optional), previous sequences, expansion activities.

**TAKE NOTE:** "His son" is used instead of Isaac to be more acceptable to Muslim students. Note subtle differences between: "put on" and "lay on"; use of "him"; "throw away" (Sequence #1) and "put away."

1. Go with your son to the mountain.
2. Take out your knife.
3. Cut some wood.
4. Put away your knife.
5. Carry the wood to the altar.
6. Lay the wood on the altar.
7. Take out your rope.
8. Tie up your son.
9. Lay him on the altar.
10. Take out your knife again.
11. God says, "Stop!"

## TEACHING THE SEQUENCE STEP BY STEP

### A. SET UP THE PROPS (1–2 minutes)

### B. TPR NEW VOCABULARY (10–15 minutes)
**Verbs:** put away, lay, tie up, says
**Vocabulary:** son, mountain, God, him

### C. MODEL (5 minutes)
1) Everyone is observing you.
2) Read and act out the Bible Sequence several times.

### D. TOGETHER (5 minutes)
1) "Now you are going to do this with me."

### E. HESITATE (5 minutes)
1) Say each line, but you hesitate before performing.

### F. JUMBLE (5 minutes)
1) Give commands from the text in random order.

### G. READING AND WRITING (15 minutes)
1) Students now open their books to the sequence pictures.
2) Read Sequence #2 to them. They follow the pictures.
3) Students write the sequence lines below each picture.
4) Read the sequence two or three times. Students follow the written words.
5) TPR the pictures.
6) Pause for questions and to point out language subtleties.

### H. SPEAKING (10 minutes)
1) Do **Backward Build-up** for each line of the sequence.
2) Repeat the Bible Sequence in normal speech. Speak slowly.
3) Listen for major pronunciation problems.

### I. ROLE REVERSAL (10 minutes)
1) One or more students direct you through the sequence.
2) Assign sequence lines to students.
3) One student directs another.

### J. SMALL-GROUP WORK (15–20 minutes)
1) Students direct each other. Books are closed, except for the speaker's.
2) Combine these techniques: **Hesitate, Jumble** and TPR the pictures.
3) Circulate around the room to encourage and help.

### EXPANSION ACTIVITIES: (Refer to Chapter 5.)

Recommended for early sequences:
- Questions from Beginning Lessons:
  What is this? Is this_____? Where is _____? Who has _____?
- Substitution drills
- Question-chain drills
- Jumble and match pictures
- Deliberate mistakes

### PRONUNCIATION:

Follow the suggestions given in Chapter 8. Focus on the sounds, not on teaching the vocabulary in this section.

### WORD ORDER:

Follow suggestions given for this exercise on page 70.

Answers:

1) Take out your knife.
2) Put your knife away.
3) Carry the wood to the alter.
4) Go with your son to the mountain.
5) Take out your rope.

### FILL IN THE BLANK:

Follow suggestions given for this exercise on page 70.

Answers:

1) knife
2) with
3) the, the
4) up
5) Take

## VOCABULARY SUMMARY:

| Verbs | Nouns |
|-------|-------|
| go | mountain |
| take | knife |
| cut | wood |
| put | altar |
| carry | rope |
| lay | son |
| tie | God |
| stop | |
| says | |

**Other vocabulary:** your, some, again, away, up, on

## SENTENCE FORMATION:
Explain the example. Give other examples, if necessary. When appropriate, explain tense and person changes that occur in this exercise.

## READING:
1) True/False: 1-F, 2-F, 3-T, 4-F, 5-T.

2) Discussion section: Abraham is the father of our faith. God promised to bless the world through Abraham's seed. (Christ) God's Son will come through the nation of Israel.

   a) Read together Genesis 12:2,3: "I will make you [Abraham] a great nation, and I will bless you. I will make you famous, and you will be a blessing to others.... And all the people on earth will be blessed through you."

   b) Question for students: Who does God bless?

   c) Additional verses: Romans 4:13–17; Galatians 3:29.

# Sequence #3: Moses and the Burning Bush (Exodus 3:2–6; 4:2–4)

**REVIEW WITH STUDENTS:** Choose some of the following items for review before beginning this sequence: vocabulary, questions, alphabet, numbers, colors, survival texts (optional), previous sequences, expansion activities.

**TAKE NOTE:** Consider how to illustrate lines 1, 7 and 9. If necessary, have the students look at the pictures as you act out the sequence for the first time.

1. Look at the burning bush.
2. Go closer to the bush.
3. God says, "Stop. Don't go any closer."
4. Bend down and take off your sandals.
5. Cover your face with both hands.
6. God says, "Throw your stick on the ground."
7. The stick changes into a snake.
8. God says, "Reach out and pick up the snake."
9. The snake changes back into a stick.
10. Hold the stick with both hands.

## *TEACHING THE SEQUENCE STEP BY STEP*

### A. SET UP THE PROPS (1–2 minutes)

### B. TPR NEW VOCABULARY (10–15 minutes)
**Verbs:** changes, reach out
**Vocabulary:** burning, closer, snake, any, into

### C. MODEL (5 minutes)
1) Everyone is observing you.
2) Read and act out the Bible Sequence several times.

### D. TOGETHER (5 minutes)
1) "Now you are going to do this with me."

### E. HESITATE (5 minutes)
1) Say each line, but you hesitate before performing.

### F. JUMBLE (5 minutes)
1) Give commands from the text in random order.

### G. READING AND WRITING (15 minutes)
1) Students now open their books to the sequence pictures.
2) Read Sequence #3 to them. They follow the pictures.
3) Students write the sequence lines below each picture.
4) Read the sequence two or three times. Students follow the written words.
5) TPR the pictures.
6) Pause for questions and to point out language subtleties.

### H. SPEAKING (10 minutes)
1) Do **Backward Build-up** for each line of the sequence.
2) Repeat the Bible Sequence in normal speech. Speak slowly.
3) Listen for major pronunciation problems.

### I. ROLE REVERSAL (10 minutes)
1) One or more students direct you through the sequence.
2) Assign sequence lines to students.
3) One student directs another.

### J. SMALL-GROUP WORK (15–20 minutes)
1) Students direct each other. Books are closed, except for the speaker's.
2) Combine these techniques: **Hesitate, Jumble** and TPR the pictures.
3) Circulate around the room to encourage and help.

### EXPANSION ACTIVITIES: (Refer to Chapter 5.)

Recommended for early sequences:
- Questions from Beginning Lessons:
  What is this? Is this_____? Where is _____? Who has _____?
- Substitution drills
- Question-chain drills
- Jumble and match pictures
- Deliberate mistakes

### PRONUNCIATION:

Follow the suggestions given in Chapter 8. Focus on the sounds, not on teaching the vocabulary in this section.

### WORD ORDER:

Follow suggestions given for this exercise on page 70.
Answers:
1) Go closer to the bush.
2) Cover your face.
3) The stick changes into a snake.
4) Stop. Don't go any closer.
5) Reach out and pick up the snake.

### FILL IN THE BLANK:

Follow suggestions given for this exercise on page 70.
Answers:
1) your
2) with
3) closer
4) Look
5) says

## VOCABULARY SUMMARY:

| Verbs | Nouns |
|-------|-------|
| look (at) | bush |
| says | sandals |
| stop | face |
| take | Lord |
| cover | stick |
| bend | snake |
| throw | hands |
| hold | ground |
| changes | back |

**Other vocabulary:** don't, off, on, out, down, your, any, closer, into, both

## SENTENCE FORMATION:
Explain the example. Give other examples, if necessary. When appropriate, explain tense and person changes that occur in this exercise.

## READING:
1) True/False: 1-F, 2-F, 3-T, 4-F, 5-T.

2) Discussion section: Moses states that the Messiah will come through the tribe of Judah (Deuteronomy 18:15). During the event of this sequence, the Lord reveals Himself as the Great "I AM."

   a) Read together Exodus 3:13,14: "What if the people say, 'What is his name?' What should I tell them?" Then God says to Moses, "I AM WHO I AM. When you go to the people of Israel, tell them, 'I AM sent me to you.'"

   b) Question for students: What is God's name?

   c) Additional verses: John 8:58; Matthew 21:11; John 7:40; John 11:25–27.

# Sequence #4: David and Goliath (1 Samuel 17:38–50)

**REVIEW WITH STUDENTS:** Choose some of the following items for review before beginning this sequence: vocabulary, questions, alphabet, numbers, colors, survival texts (optional), previous sequences, expansion activities.

**TAKE NOTE:** Two items are introduced: 1) the future tense with "go" ("You're going to fight Goliath."); 2) the possessive using the apostrophe ("king's armor").

1. You're going to fight Goliath.
2. Try on the king's armor.
3. The king's armor is too big.
4. Take off the armor.
5. Pick up five smooth stones.
6. Put them in your bag.
7. Grab your sling.
8. Run to meet Goliath.
9. Take a stone out of your bag.
10. Put it in the sling.
11. Throw it!
12. The stone hits Goliath. He dies.

## *TEACHING THE SEQUENCE STEP BY STEP*

### A. SET UP THE PROPS (1–2 minutes)

### B. TPR NEW VOCABULARY (10–15 minutes)
**Verbs:** are going, fight, try on, meet, hits, dies
**Vocabulary:** king's, armor, too, them, smooth, Goliath

### C. MODEL (5 minutes)
1) Everyone is observing you.
2) Read and act out the Bible Sequence several times.

### D. TOGETHER (5 minutes)
1) "Now you are going to do this with me."

### E. HESITATE (5 minutes)
1) Say each line, but you hesitate before performing.

### F. JUMBLE (5 minutes)
1) Give commands from the text in random order.

### G. READING AND WRITING (15 minutes)
1) Students now open their books to the sequence pictures.
2) Read Sequence #4 to them. They follow the pictures.
3) Students write the sequence lines below each picture.
4) Read the sequence two or three times. Students follow the written words.
5) TPR the pictures.
6) Pause for questions and to point out language subtleties.

### H. SPEAKING (10 minutes)
1) Do **Backward Build-up** for each line of the sequence.
2) Repeat the Bible Sequence in normal speech. Speak slowly.
3) Listen for major pronunciation problems.

### I. ROLE REVERSAL (10 minutes)
1) One or more students direct you through the sequence.
2) Assign sequence lines to students.
3) One student directs another.

### J. SMALL-GROUP WORK (15–20 minutes)
1) Students direct each other. Books are closed, except for the speaker's.
2) Combine these techniques: **Hesitate, Jumble** and TPR the pictures.
3) Circulate around the room to encourage and help.

### EXPANSION ACTIVITIES: (Refer to Chapter 5.)

Recommended for early sequences:
- Questions from Beginning Lessons:
  What is this? Is this_____? Where is _____? Who has _____?
- Substitution drills
- Question-chain drills
- Jumble and match pictures
- Deliberate mistakes

Are students ready for more Expansion Activities? (Refer to pages 80–84.)

### PRONUNCIATION:
Follow the suggestions given in Chapter 8. Focus on the sounds, not on teaching the vocabulary in this section.

### WORD ORDER:
Follow suggestions given for this exercise on page 70.
Answers:
1) Pick up five smooth stones.
2) Take the armor off.
3) You're going to fight Goliath.
4) Put them in your bag.
5) The king's armor is too big.

### FILL IN THE BLANK:
Follow suggestions given for this exercise on page 70.
Answers:
1) in
2) Take
3) king's
4) to
5) out

## VOCABULARY SUMMARY:

| Verbs | Nouns |
|---|---|
| are going | armor |
| fight | stones |
| try (on) | bag |
| pick | sling |
| put | Goliath |
| grab | |
| run | |
| meet | |
| take | |
| throw | |
| hits | |
| dies | |

**Other vocabulary:** you, he, king's, five, smooth, your, it, them, up, in

## SENTENCE FORMATION:

Explain the example. Give other examples, if necessary. When appropriate, explain tense and person changes that occur in this exercise.

## READING:

1) True/False: 1-T, 2-F, 3-F, 4-F, 5-T.

2) Discussion section: The Messiah will come through David's family. Jesus is the son of David as well as David's Lord.

   a) Read together Luke 1:31–33: "Listen! You will become pregnant and give birth to a son, and you will name him Jesus. He will be great and will be called the Son of the Most High. The Lord God will give him the throne of King David, his ancestor. He will rule over the people of Jacob forever, and his kingdom will never end."

   b) Question for students: Who has the throne of David?

   c) Additional verses: Matthew 1:1; 2 Timothy 2:8; Matthew 22:44, 45.

## Sequence #5: Jonah Is Angry (Jonah 4:1–11)

**REVIEW WITH STUDENTS:** Choose some of the following items for review before beginning this sequence: vocabulary, questions, alphabet, numbers, colors, survival texts (optional), previous sequences, expansion activities.

**TAKE NOTE:** The present continuous tense is introduced ("You are sitting in your house."). After learning the sequence, practice the present continuous with previously learned verbs ("I am walking."). Also, notice the emphasis on the verb "are."

1. You are sitting in your house.
2. You are angry.
3. Go outside.
4. Sit down under a tree.
5. Stay in the shade.
6. You are hot.
7. You are thirsty.
8. You are angry at God.
9. God says, "Be quiet!"
10. "Listen to me."

## *TEACHING THE SEQUENCE STEP BY STEP*

### A. SET UP THE PROPS (1–2 minutes)

### B. TPR NEW VOCABULARY (10–15 minutes)
**Verbs:** stay, be (quiet), listen
**Vocabulary:** outside, shade, thirsty, angry, hot, to me

### C. MODEL (5 minutes)
1) Everyone is observing you.
2) Read and act out the Bible Sequence several times.

### D. TOGETHER (5 minutes)
1) "Now you are going to do this with me."

### E. HESITATE (5 minutes)
1) Say each line, but you hesitate before performing.

### F. JUMBLE (5 minutes)
1) Give commands from the text in random order.

### G. READING AND WRITING (15 minutes)
1) Students now open their books to the sequence pictures.
2) Read Sequence #5 to them. They follow the pictures.
3) Students write the sequence lines below each picture.
4) Read the sequence two or three times. Students follow the written words.
5) TPR the pictures.
6) Pause for questions and to point out language subtleties.

### H. SPEAKING (10 minutes)
1) Do **Backward Build-up** for each line of the sequence.
2) Repeat the Bible Sequence in normal speech. Speak slowly.
3) Listen for major pronunciation problems.

### I. ROLE REVERSAL (10 minutes)
1) One or more students direct you through the sequence.
2) Assign sequence lines to students.
3) One student directs another.

### J. SMALL-GROUP WORK (15–20 minutes)
1) Students direct each other. Books are closed, except for the speaker's.
2) Combine these techniques: **Hesitate, Jumble** and TPR the pictures.
3) Circulate around the room to encourage and help.

### EXPANSION ACTIVITIES: (Refer to Chapter 5.)

Are students ready for more Expansion Activities? (Refer to pages 80–84.)

### PRONUNCIATION:

Follow the suggestions given in Chapter 8. Focus on the sounds, not on teaching the vocabulary in this section.

### WORD ORDER:

Follow suggestions given for this exercise on page 70.

Answers:

1) Sit down under a tree.
2) You are thirsty.
3) Listen to God.
4) Stay in the shade.
5) You are sitting in the house.

### FILL IN THE BLANK:

Follow suggestions given for this exercise on page 70.

Answers:

1) You
2) are
3) shade
4) to
5) under

## VOCABULARY SUMMARY:

| **Verbs** | **Nouns** |
| --- | --- |
| are sitting | tree |
| go | shade |
| sit | God |
| stay | house |
| listen | |
| says | |

**Other vocabulary:** you, very, unhappy, angry, under, in, at, hot, thirsty, inside, outside

## SENTENCE FORMATION:
Explain the example. Give other examples, if necessary. When appropriate, explain tense and person changes that occur in this exercise.

## READING:
1) True/False: 1-F, 2-T, 3-T, 4-T, 5-F.

2) Discussion section: Jonah's unwillingness to forgive others is contrasted with God's mercy. The sign of Jonah is an important foreshadowing of the resurrection of Jesus Christ.

   a) Read together Matthew 12:40: "Jonah was in the stomach of the big fish for three days and three nights. In the same way, the Son of Man will be in the grave three days and three nights."

   b) Question for students: Who is the Son of Man?

   c) Additional verses: John 11:25; John 2:19–22; John 6:39,40; John 10:17,18.

# ⭐ Sequence #6: Jesus' Birth: Wise Men Visit (Matthew 2:1–11)

**REVIEW WITH STUDENTS:** Choose some of the following items for review before beginning this sequence: vocabulary, questions, alphabet, numbers, colors, survival texts (optional), previous sequences, expansion activities.

**TAKE NOTE:** Demonstrate the difference between "his" and "him"; also note "for him," "to him."

1. You're going to see the baby Jesus.
2. You see his star.
3. Follow his star.
4. Go to the house.
5. Knock on the door.
6. Go inside.
7. Look at the baby Jesus.
8. Hold him.
9. Now, put him down.
10. You have a gift for him.
11. Open the gift.
12. Give it to him.
13. You're very happy. Smile.

## TEACHING THE SEQUENCE STEP BY STEP

### A. SET UP THE PROPS (1–2 minutes)

### B. TPR NEW VOCABULARY (10–15 minutes)
**Verbs:** see, knock, open, smile
**Vocabulary:** baby, Jesus, door, inside, now, him, very

### C. MODEL (5 minutes)
1) Everyone is observing you.
2) Read and act out the Bible Sequence several times.

### D. TOGETHER (5 minutes)
1) "Now you are going to do this with me."

### E. HESITATE (5 minutes)
1) Say each line, but you hesitate before performing.

### F. JUMBLE (5 minutes)
1) Give commands from the text in random order.

### G. READING AND WRITING (15 minutes)
1) Students now open their books to the sequence pictures.
2) Read Sequence #6 to them. They follow the pictures.
3) Students write the sequence lines below each picture.
4) Read the sequence two or three times. Students follow the written words.
5) TPR the pictures.
6) Pause for questions and to point out language subtleties.

### H. SPEAKING (10 minutes)
1) Do **Backward Build-up** for each line of the sequence.
2) Repeat the Bible Sequence in normal speech. Speak slowly.
3) Listen for major pronunciation problems.

### I. ROLE REVERSAL (10 minutes)
1) One or more students direct you through the sequence.
2) Assign sequence lines to students.
3) One student directs another.

### J. SMALL-GROUP WORK (15–20 minutes)
1) Students direct each other. Books are closed, except for the speaker's.
2) Combine these techniques: **Hesitate, Jumble** and TPR the pictures.
3) Circulate around the room to encourage and help.

### EXPANSION ACTIVITIES: (Refer to Chapter 5.)

Are students ready for more Expansion Activities? (Refer to pages 80–84.)

### PRONUNCIATION:

Follow the suggestions given in Chapter 8. Focus on the sounds, not on teaching the vocabulary in this section.

### WORD ORDER:

Follow suggestions given for this exercise on page 70.

Answers:

1) Follow his star.
2) You're very happy.
3) You have a gift for him.
4) Knock on the door.
5) Put him down.

### FILL IN THE BLANK:

Follow suggestions given for this exercise on page 70.

Answers:

1) Open
2) star
3) the
4) to
5) to

## VOCABULARY SUMMARY:

| Verbs | Nouns |
|---|---|
| are going | baby Jesus |
| see | star |
| follow | house |
| knock | door |
| go | gift |
| look | |
| hold | |
| put | |
| have | |
| open | |
| give | |
| are | |
| smile | |

**Other vocabulary:** his, him, very, happy, on, at, down, you, now, for, it

## SENTENCE FORMATION:
Explain the example. Give other examples, if necessary. When appropriate, explain tense and person changes that occur in this exercise.

## READING:
1) True/False: 1-F, 2-T, 3-F, 4-T, 5-T.

2) Discussion section: Jesus was born King of the Jews. The King was rejected by His people (John 1:11).

   a) Read together John 18: 33, 37: "Are you the king of the Jews?" Jesus answered, "You say that I am a king. That is true. I was born for this: to tell people about the truth. That is why I came into the world. And everyone who belongs to the truth listens to me."

   b) Question for students: Is Jesus a king?

   c) Additional verses: Revelation 19:15,16.

Sequence #7: Wedding at Cana (John 2:1–11)

**REVIEW WITH STUDENTS:** Choose some of the following items for review before beginning this sequence: vocabulary, questions, alphabet, numbers, colors, survival texts (optional), previous sequences, expansion activities.

**TAKE NOTE:** Emphasize the third-person singular "he." Point out/practice addition of "s" to singular verbs (says, pours, smells, tastes). Note the reflexive pronoun "himself" in forming sentences. "Oh, no!" expresses disappointment; "Look!" expresses surprise.

1. You're going to get some wine.
2. Fill up this pitcher with wine.
3. Oh, no! The barrel is empty!
4. Jesus says, "Fill up that barrel with water."
5. Now, take out some water.
6. Look! The water has changed into wine.
7. Take some to the head waiter.
8. He pours himself a glass of wine.
9. He smells it.
10. He tastes it.
11. He says, "This wine is very good!"

## TEACHING THE SEQUENCE STEP BY STEP

### A. SET UP THE PROPS (1–2 minutes)

### B. TPR NEW VOCABULARY (10–15 minutes)
**Verbs:** has changed, taste
**Vocabulary:** barrel, empty, waiter, "Oh, no!," himself, good

### C. MODEL (5 minutes)
1) Everyone is observing you.
2) Read and act out the Bible Sequence several times.

### D. TOGETHER (5 minutes)
1) "Now you are going to do this with me."

### E. HESITATE (5 minutes)
1) Say each line, but you hesitate before performing.

### F. JUMBLE (5 minutes)
1) Give commands from the text in random order.

### G. READING AND WRITING (15 minutes)
1) Students now open their books to the sequence pictures.
2) Read Sequence #7 to them. They follow the pictures.
3) Students write the sequence lines below each picture.
4) Read the sequence two or three times. Students follow the written words.
5) TPR the pictures.
6) Pause for questions and to point out language subtleties.

### H. SPEAKING (10 minutes)
1) Do **Backward Build-up** for each line of the sequence.
2) Repeat the Bible Sequence in normal speech. Speak slowly.
3) Listen for major pronunciation problems.

### I. ROLE REVERSAL (10 minutes)
1) One or more students direct you through the sequence.
2) Assign sequence lines to students.
3) One student directs another.

### J. SMALL-GROUP WORK (15–20 minutes)
1) Students direct each other. Books are closed, except for the speaker's.
2) Combine these techniques: **Hesitate, Jumble** and TPR the pictures.
3) Circulate around the room to encourage and help.

### EXPANSION ACTIVITIES: (Refer to Chapter 5.)

Are students ready for more Expansion Activities? (Refer to pages 80–84.)

### PRONUNCIATION:

Follow the suggestions given in Chapter 8. Focus on the sounds, not on teaching the vocabulary in this section.

### WORD ORDER:

Follow suggestions given for this exercise on page 70.

Answers:

1) Take some to the head waiter.
2) The barrel is empty.
3) Fill up this pitcher with wine.
4) You're going to get some wine.
5) Now, take some water out.

### FILL IN THE BLANK:

Follow suggestions given for this exercise on page 70.

Answers:

1) that, with
2) is
3) very
4) take, out
5) it

## VOCABULARY SUMMARY:

| Verbs | Nouns |
|---|---|
| are going | wine |
| get | pitcher |
| fill | barrel |
| is | water |
| take | a glass |
| has changed | waiter |
| pour | |
| smell | |
| taste | |
| is | |

**Other vocabulary:** he, this, that, head, with, "Oh, no!", empty, some, very, good, himself, up, out, into

## SENTENCE FORMATION:

Explain the example. Give other examples, if necessary. When appropriate, explain tense and person changes that occur in this exercise.

## READING:

1) True/False: 1-T, 2-T, 3-F, 4-F, 5-T.

2) Discussion section: Jesus performed miracles so that people would believe in Him.

   a) Read together John 14:11: "Believe me when I say that I am in the Father and the Father is in me. Or believe because of the miracles I have done."

   b) Question for students: Why did Jesus do miracles?

   c) Additional verses: Mark 11:4–6; John 1:48,49.

## Sequence #8: Feeding of the 5,000 (John 6:5–14)

**REVIEW WITH STUDENTS:** Choose some of the following items for review before beginning this sequence: vocabulary, questions, alphabet, numbers, colors, survival texts (optional), previous sequences, expansion activities.

**TAKE NOTE:** TPR the word "before" ("Before you stand up, point to the table."). "Wow!" expresses amazement; "What a …" notes something special.

1. You're going to see Jesus today.
2. Before you leave, take out your lunch.
3. Wrap the biscuits and fish in paper.
4. Put them in a bag.
5. Leave the house. Listen to Jesus speak.
6. Now, give your lunch to Jesus.
7. Jesus says, "Give the bread and fish to the people."
8. Pick up the leftover pieces of food.
9. Put them in the baskets.
10. You fill twelve large baskets.
11. Give the baskets back to Jesus.
12. Wow! What a day it was!

## *TEACHING THE SEQUENCE STEP BY STEP*

### A. SET UP THE PROPS (1–2 minutes)

### B. TPR NEW VOCABULARY (10–15 minutes)
**Verbs:** leave, was, wrap, listen, speak
**Vocabulary:** today, before, lunch, biscuits, bread, people, leftover, pieces, food, large, "Wow!", "What a day!"

### C. MODEL (5 minutes)
1) Everyone is observing you.
2) Read and act out the Bible Sequence several times.

### D. TOGETHER (5 minutes)
1) "Now you are going to do this with me."

### E. HESITATE (5 minutes)
1) Say each line, but you hesitate before performing.

### F. JUMBLE (5 minutes)
1) Give commands from the text in random order.

### G. READING AND WRITING (15 minutes)
1) Students now open their books to the sequence pictures.
2) Read Sequence #8 to them. They follow the pictures.
3) Students write the sequence lines below each picture.
4) Read the sequence two or three times. Students follow the written words.
5) TPR the pictures.
6) Pause for questions and to point out language subtleties.

### H. SPEAKING (10 minutes)
1) Do **Backward Build-up** for each line of the sequence.
2) Repeat the Bible Sequence in normal speech. Speak slowly.
3) Listen for major pronunciation problems.

### I. ROLE REVERSAL (10 minutes)
1) One or more students direct you through the sequence.
2) Assign sequence lines to students.
3) One student directs another.

### J. SMALL-GROUP WORK (15–20 minutes)
1) Students direct each other. Books are closed, except for the speaker's.
2) Combine these techniques: **Hesitate, Jumble** and TPR the pictures.
3) Circulate around the room to encourage and help.

## EXPANSION ACTIVITIES: (Refer to Chapter 5.)

Are students ready for more Expansion Activities? (Refer to pages 80–84.)

## PRONUNCIATION:

Follow the suggestions given in Chapter 8. Focus on the sounds, not on teaching the vocabulary in this section.

## WORD ORDER:

Follow suggestions given for this exercise on page 70.

Answers:

1) Wrap the biscuits and fish in paper.
2) Leave the house.
3) Now, give your lunch to Jesus.
4) Put them in the baskets.
5) Give the baskets back to Jesus.

## FILL IN THE BLANK:

Follow suggestions given for this exercise on page 70.

Answers:

1) them
2) going
3) the, of
4) you, your
5) fill

## VOCABULARY SUMMARY:

| Verbs | Nouns |
|---|---|
| are going | Jesus |
| see | biscuits |
| leave | fish |
| take | paper |
| wrap | bag |
| put | people |
| listen | pieces |
| speak | food |
| pick | baskets |
| fill | house |
| give | day |
| was | |

**Other vocabulary:** today, before, you, your, them, now, out, in, what, back, "Wow!"

## SENTENCE FORMATION:
Explain the example. Give other examples, if necessary. When appropriate, explain tense and person changes that occur in this exercise.

## READING:
1) True/False: 1-T, 2-T, 3-T, 4-F, 5-T.

2) Discussion section: Bread and water are important symbols in the New Testament. Jesus is the bread and water of life.

   a) Read together John 6:35: Then Jesus said, "I am the bread of life. He who comes to me will never be hungry. He who believes in me will never be thirsty."

   b) Question for students: What is the bread and the water?

   c) Additional verses: John 4:13,14; John 7:37–39.

## Sequence #9: Healing of a Blind Man (John 9:1–15)

**REVIEW WITH STUDENTS:** Choose some of the following items for review before beginning this sequence: vocabulary, questions, alphabet, numbers, colors, survival texts (optional), previous sequences, expansion activities.

**TAKE NOTE:** "Jump for joy" is an expression of great happiness.

1. You can't see. You are blind.
2. One day you meet Jesus.
3. Jesus bends down and makes mud.
4. He puts the mud on your eyes.
5. He tells you, "Go and wash."
6. Dry your face.
7. Rub your eyes with both hands.
8. Now, open your eyes.
9. You can see!
10. Jump for joy!

## TEACHING THE SEQUENCE STEP BY STEP

### A. SET UP THE PROPS (1–2 minutes)

### B. TPR NEW VOCABULARY (10–15 minutes)
**Verbs:** makes, tells, wash, dry
**Vocabulary:** blind, day, dirt, mud, eyes, joy

### C. MODEL (5 minutes)
1) Everyone is observing you.
2) Read and act out the Bible Sequence several times.

### D. TOGETHER (5 minutes)
1) "Now you are going to do this with me."

### E. HESITATE (5 minutes)
1) Say each line, but you hesitate before performing.

### F. JUMBLE (5 minutes)
1) Give commands from the text in random order.

### G. READING AND WRITING (15 minutes)
1) Students now open their books to the sequence pictures.
2) Read Sequence #9 to them. They follow the pictures.
3) Students write the sequence lines below each picture.
4) Read the sequence two or three times. Students follow the written words.
5) TPR the pictures.
6) Pause for questions and to point out language subtleties.

### H. SPEAKING (10 minutes)
1) Do **Backward Build-up** for each line of the sequence.
2) Repeat the Bible Sequence in normal speech. Speak slowly.
3) Listen for major pronunciation problems.

### I. ROLE REVERSAL (10 minutes)
1) One or more students direct you through the sequence.
2) Assign sequence lines to students.
3) One student directs another.

### J. SMALL-GROUP WORK (15–20 minutes)
1) Students direct each other. Books are closed, except for the speaker's.
2) Combine these techniques: **Hesitate, Jumble** and TPR the pictures.
3) Circulate around the room to encourage and help.

### EXPANSION ACTIVITIES: (Refer to Chapter 5.)

Are students ready for more Expansion Activities? (Refer to pages 80–84.)

### PRONUNCIATION:

Follow the suggestions given in Chapter 8. Focus on the sounds, not on teaching the vocabulary in this section.

### WORD ORDER:

Follow suggestions given for this exercise on page 70.

Answers:

1) You can't see. You are blind.
2) He puts the mud on your eyes.
3) He tells you, "Go and wash."
4) Rub your eyes with both hands.
5) Now, open your eyes.

### FILL IN THE BLANK:

Follow suggestions given for this exercise on page 70.

Answers:

1) you
2) bends, mud
3) your
4) He
5) Rub

## VOCABULARY SUMMARY:

| Verbs | Nouns |
|-------|-------|
| can | Jesus |
| can't | mud |
| see | eyes |
| meet | face |
| bends | hands |
| makes | day |
| tells | joy |
| puts | |
| go | |
| wash | |
| dry | |
| rub | |
| open | |
| jump | |

**Other vocabulary:** You, one, on, and, your, in, now, I, for

## SENTENCE FORMATION:

Explain the example. Give other examples, if necessary. When appropriate, explain tense and person changes that occur in this exercise.

## READING:

1) True/False: 1-T, 2-F, 3-T, 4-T, 5-F.

2) Discussion section: Accepting our own blindness (sin) is the first step in coming to know Christ.

   a) Read together John 9:40,41: "They asked, 'What? Are you saying that we are blind, too?' Jesus said, 'If you were really blind, you would not be guilty of sin. But now that you say you can see, your guilt remains.'"

   b) Question for students: Who is blind?

   c) Additional verses: John 8:12; Luke 18:9–14; 1 John 1:8.

Sequence #10: The Sower (Mark 4:3–8)

**REVIEW WITH STUDENTS:** Choose some of the following items for review before beginning this sequence: vocabulary, questions, alphabet, numbers, colors, survival texts (optional), previous sequences, expansion activities.

**TAKE NOTE:** Practice using these adjectives: some, several, each and other. Demonstrate different uses of the word "water" in lines 9 and 10.

1. You're going to plant some seed.
2. Some seed falls on the road.
3. Other seed falls on rocky ground.
4. Other seed falls among weeds.
5. Make several holes in good ground.
6. Put some seed in each hole.
7. Cover the holes with dirt.
8. Press down the dirt with both hands.
9. Fill a can with water.
10. Water the seeds.
11. Where is the seed growing?

## *TEACHING THE SEQUENCE STEP BY STEP*

### A. SET UP THE PROPS (1–2 minutes)

### B. TPR NEW VOCABULARY (10–15 minutes)
**Verbs:** plant, falls, press, water
**Vocabulary:** road, rocky, ground, among, weeds, each, dirt, can

### C. MODEL (5 minutes)
1) Everyone is observing you.
2) Read and act out the Bible Sequence several times.

### D. TOGETHER (5 minutes)
1) "Now you are going to do this with me."

### E. HESITATE (5 minutes)
1) Say each line, but you hesitate before performing.

### F. JUMBLE (5 minutes)
1) Give commands from the text in random order.

### G. READING AND WRITING (15 minutes)
1) Students now open their books to the sequence pictures.
2) Read Sequence #10 to them. They follow the pictures.
3) Students write the sequence lines below each picture.
4) Read the sequence two or three times. Students follow the written words.
5) TPR the pictures.
6) Pause for questions and to point out language subtleties.

### H. SPEAKING (10 minutes)
1) Do **Backward Build-up** for each line of the sequence.
2) Repeat the Bible Sequence in normal speech. Speak slowly.
3) Listen for major pronunciation problems.

### I. ROLE REVERSAL (10 minutes)
1) One or more students direct you through the sequence.
2) Assign sequence lines to students.
3) One student directs another.

### J. SMALL-GROUP WORK (15–20 minutes)
1) Students direct each other. Books are closed, except for the speaker's.
2) Combine these techniques: **Hesitate, Jumble** and TPR the pictures.
3) Circulate around the room to encourage and help.

**EXPANSION ACTIVITIES: (Refer to Chapter 5.)**

Are students ready for more Expansion Activities? (Refer to pages 80–84.)

**PRONUNCIATION:**
Follow the suggestions given in Chapter 8. Focus on the sounds, not on teaching the vocabulary in this section.

**WORD ORDER:**
Follow suggestions given for this exercise on page 70.
Answers:
1) Cover the holes with dirt.
2) Press down the dirt with both hands.
3) Make several holes in good ground.
4) Put a seed in each hole.
5) Water the seeds.

**FILL IN THE BLANK:**
Follow suggestions given for this exercise on page 70.
Answers:
1) going, some
2) with
3) falls
4) Fill
5) Where

**VOCABULARY SUMMARY:**

| Verbs | Nouns |
|---|---|
| are going | seed (s) |
| plant | hole (s) |
| falls | ground |
| make | weeds |
| put | can (pitcher) |
| cover | water |
| press | hands |
| fill | dirt |
| water | road |
| is growing | |

**Other vocabulary:** some, several, in, each, with, down, rocky, among, good, where

**SENTENCE FORMATION:**

Explain the example. Give other examples, if necessary. When appropriate, explain tense and person changes that occur in this exercise.

**READING:**

1) True/False: 1-T, 2-T, 3-F, 4-T, 5-F.

2) Discussion section: This parable is about the human heart and its response to God's message. Good ground represents people who obey the message.

a) Read together James 1:22: "Do what God's teaching says; do not just listen and do nothing. When you only sit and listen, you are fooling yourselves."

b) Question for students: What is good ground?

c) Additional verses: John 12:47–50.

# Sequence #11: The Lost Coin (Luke 15:8–9)

**REVIEW WITH STUDENTS:** Choose some of the following items for review before beginning this sequence: vocabulary, questions, alphabet, numbers, colors, survival texts (optional), previous sequences, expansion activities.

**TAKE NOTE:** "Furniture" is a category name, like cars, plants and animals.

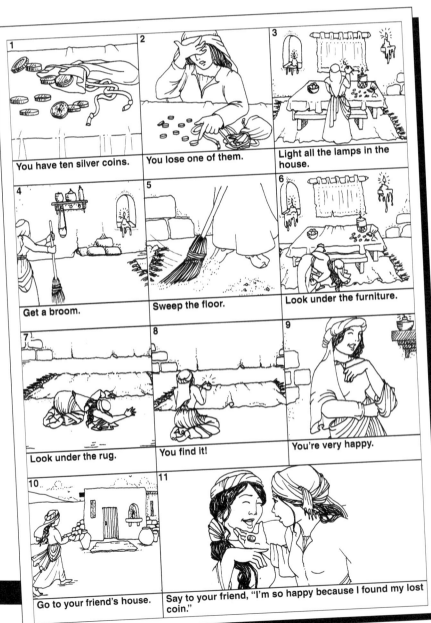

1. You have ten silver coins.
2. You lose one of them.
3. Light all the lamps in the house.
4. Get a broom.
5. Sweep the floor.
6. Look under the furniture.
7. Look under the rug.
8. You find it!
9. You're very happy.
10. Go to your friend's house.
11. Say to your friend, "I'm so happy because I found my lost coin."

## *TEACHING THE SEQUENCE STEP BY STEP*

### A. SET UP THE PROPS (1–2 minutes)

### B. TPR NEW VOCABULARY (10–15 minutes)
**Verbs:** lose, sweep, find, found, am, light
**Vocabulary:** silver, all, lamps, broom, rug, furniture, floor, my, so, because, lost

### C. MODEL (5 minutes)
1) Everyone is observing you.
2) Read and act out the Bible Sequence several times.

### D. TOGETHER (5 minutes)
1) "Now you are going to do this with me."

### E. HESITATE (5 minutes)
1) Say each line, but you hesitate before performing.

### F. JUMBLE (5 minutes)
1) Give commands from the text in random order.

### G. READING AND WRITING (15 minutes)
1) Students now open their books to the sequence pictures.
2) Read Sequence #11 to them. They follow the pictures.
3) Students write the sequence lines below each picture.
4) Read the sequence two or three times. Students follow the written words.
5) TPR the pictures.
6) Pause for questions and to point out language subtleties.

### H. SPEAKING (10 minutes)
1) Do **Backward Build-up** for each line of the sequence.
2) Repeat the Bible Sequence in normal speech. Speak slowly.
3) Listen for major pronunciation problems.

### I. ROLE REVERSAL (10 minutes)
1) One or more students direct you through the sequence.
2) Assign sequence lines to students.
3) One student directs another.

### J. SMALL-GROUP WORK (15–20 minutes)
1) Students direct each other. Books are closed, except for the speaker's.
2) Combine these techniques: **Hesitate, Jumble** and TPR the pictures.
3) Circulate around the room to encourage and help.

### EXPANSION ACTIVITIES: (Refer to Chapter 5.)

Are students ready for more Expansion Activities? (Refer to pages 80–84.)

### PRONUNCIATION:

Follow the suggestions given in Chapter 8. Focus on the sounds, not on teaching the vocabulary in this section.

### WORD ORDER:

Follow suggestions given for this exercise on page 70.

Answers:

1) You have ten silver coins.

2) Light all the lamps in the house.

3) Look under the rug.

4) You find it.

5) Go to your friend's house.

### FILL IN THE BLANK:

Follow suggestions given for this exercise on page 70.

Answers:

1) lose

2) broom

3) floor

4) under

5) very

## VOCABULARY SUMMARY:

| Verbs | Nouns |
|-------|-------|
| have | coins |
| lose | lamps |
| light | broom |
| get | house |
| sweep | rug |
| look | friend |
| found | |
| are | |
| go | |
| am | |
| say | |

**Other vocabulary:** silver, one, all, under, you, very, your, on, so, happy, I, my, lost, friend's, because, it

## SENTENCE FORMATION:

Explain the example. Give other examples, if necessary. When appropriate, explain tense and person changes that occur in this exercise.

## READING:

1) True/False: 1-T, 2-T, 3-T, 4-T, 5-T.

2) Discussion section: This parable reflects the joy of God in forgiving sinners.

   a) Read together Luke 19:10: "The Son of Man came to find lost people and save them."

   b) Question for students: What do "lost" and "saved" mean?

   c) Additional verses: John 3:16; Romans 6:23; Ephesians 2:8,9; 1 John 5:11,12.

# Sequence #12: The Hidden Treasure (Matthew 13:44)

**REVIEW WITH STUDENTS:** Choose some of the following items for review before beginning this sequence: vocabulary, questions, alphabet, numbers, colors, survival texts (optional), previous sequences, expansion activities.

**TAKE NOTE:** "Where could it be?" is a possibility question.

1. There is a treasure hidden in a field.
2. Run to the field.
3. Think. Where could it be?
4. Look behind the tree. It's not there.
5. Look under the rock. It's not there.
6. Look in the bushes. It's not there.
7. Think again. Where could it be?
8. Dig up the flowers.
9. There it is. You found it!
10. Hide the treasure again.
11. Buy the field.

## *TEACHING THE SEQUENCE STEP BY STEP*

### A. SET UP THE PROPS (1–2 minutes)

### B. TPR NEW VOCABULARY (10–15 minutes)
**Verbs:** hidden, think, dig (up), buy
**Vocabulary:** there, treasure, field, flowers, could

### C. MODEL (5 minutes)
1) Everyone is observing you.
2) Read and act out the Bible Sequence several times.

### D. TOGETHER (5 minutes)
1) "Now you are going to do this with me."

### E. HESITATE (5 minutes)
1) Say each line, but you hesitate before performing.

### F. JUMBLE (5 minutes)
1) Give commands from the text in random order.

### G. READING AND WRITING (15 minutes)
1) Students now open their books to the sequence pictures.
2) Read Sequence #12 to them. They follow the pictures.
3) Students write the sequence lines below each picture.
4) Read the sequence two or three times. Students follow the written words.
5) TPR the pictures.
6) Pause for questions and to point out language subtleties.

### H. SPEAKING (10 minutes)
1) Do **Backward Build-up** for each line of the sequence.
2) Repeat the Bible Sequence in normal speech. Speak slowly.
3) Listen for major pronunciation problems.

### I. ROLE REVERSAL (10 minutes)
1) One or more students direct you through the sequence.
2) Assign sequence lines to students.
3) One student directs another.

### J. SMALL-GROUP WORK (15–20 minutes)
1) Students direct each other. Books are closed, except for the speaker's.
2) Combine these techniques: **Hesitate, Jumble** and TPR the pictures.
3) Circulate around the room to encourage and help.

## EXPANSION ACTIVITIES: (Refer to Chapter 5.)

Are students ready for more Expansion Activities? (Refer to pages 80–84.)

## PRONUNCIATION:

Follow the suggestions given in Chapter 8. Focus on the sounds, not on teaching the vocabulary in this section.

## WORD ORDER:

Follow suggestions given for this exercise on page 70.

Answers:

1) Run to the field.
2) Where could it be?
3) It's not there.
4) Hide the treasure again.
5) Buy the field.

## FILL IN THE BLANK:

Follow suggestions given for this exercise on page 70.

Answers:

1) is
2) it
3) bushes
4) Dig
5) again

## VOCABULARY SUMMARY:

| Verbs | Nouns |
|---|---|
| is | treasure |
| run | rock |
| go | bushes |
| think | flowers |
| look | field |
| be | tree |
| dig (up) | |
| found | |
| hide | |
| buy | |

**Other vocabulary:** behind, it, there, under, in, you, could, it's, not, again

## SENTENCE FORMATION:

Explain the example. Give other examples, if necessary. When appropriate, explain tense and person changes that occur in this exercise.

## READING:

1) True/False: 1-F, 2-T, 3-T, 4-F, 5-T.

2) Discussion section: God and His kingdom should be of the greatest possible value to us.

   a) Read together Philippians 3:7,8: "At one time all these things were important to me. But now I think those things are worth nothing because of Christ. Not only those things, but I think that all things are worth nothing compared with the greatness of knowing Christ Jesus my Lord..." (Saint Paul).

   b) Question for students: What was important to Saint Paul? Why?

   c) Additional verses: 1 Corinthians 8:6; 2 Corinthians 5:15; Philippians 1:21.

## Sequence #13: The Good Samaritan (Luke 10:30–37)

**REVIEW WITH STUDENTS:** Choose some of the following items for review before beginning this sequence: vocabulary, questions, alphabet, numbers, colors, survival texts (optional), previous sequences, expansion activities.

**TAKE NOTE:** The next three sequences use the present continuous tense (be + verb + ing). Also introduced is the future tense with "will." Once these are learned, use these tenses with TPR work (Teacher asks: "What will you do?"; student responds, "I will stand up.").

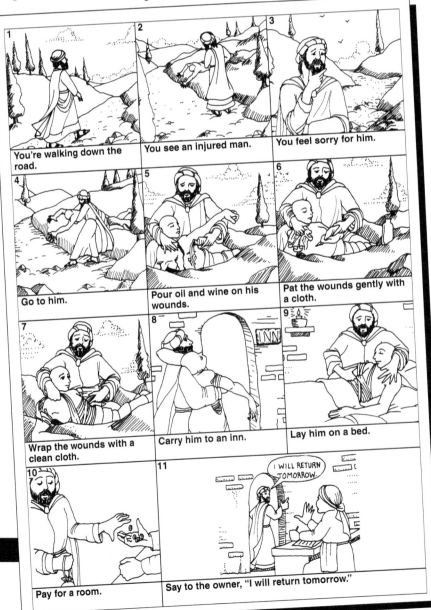

## *TEACHING THE SEQUENCE STEP BY STEP*

### A. SET UP THE PROPS (1–2 minutes)

### B. TPR NEW VOCABULARY (10–15 minutes)
**Verbs:** pat, pay, will return
**Vocabulary:** injured, man, sorry, wounds, gently, clean, inn, bed, pay, room, owner, tomorrow

### C. MODEL (5 minutes)
1) Everyone is observing you.
2) Read and act out the Bible Sequence several times.

### D. TOGETHER (5 minutes)
1) "Now you are going to do this with me."

### E. HESITATE (5 minutes)
1) Say each line, but you hesitate before performing.

### F. JUMBLE (5 minutes)
1) Give commands from the text in random order.

### G. READING AND WRITING (15 minutes)
1) Students now open their books to the sequence pictures.
2) Read Sequence #13 to them. They follow the pictures.
3) Students write the sequence lines below each picture.
4) Read the sequence two or three times. Students follow the written words.
5) TPR the pictures.
6) Pause for questions and to point out language subtleties.

### H. SPEAKING (10 minutes)
1) Do **Backward Build-up** for each line of the sequence.
2) Repeat the Bible Sequence in normal speech. Speak slowly.
3) Listen for major pronunciation problems.

### I. ROLE REVERSAL (10 minutes)
1) One or more students direct you through the sequence.
2) Assign sequence lines to students.
3) One student directs another.

### J. SMALL-GROUP WORK (15–20 minutes)
1) Students direct each other. Books are closed, except for the speaker's.
2) Combine these techniques: **Hesitate, Jumble** and TPR the pictures.
3) Circulate around the room to encourage and help.

## EXPANSION ACTIVITIES: (Refer to Chapter 5.)

Are students ready for more Expansion Activities? (Refer to pages 80–84.)

## PRONUNCIATION:
Follow the suggestions given in Chapter 8. Focus on the sounds, not on teaching the vocabulary in this section.

## WORD ORDER:
Follow suggestions given for this exercise on page 70.
Answers:
1) You feel sorry for him.
2) Pour oil and wine on his wounds.
3) You're walking down the road.
4) Carry him to an inn.
5) Pay for a room.

## FILL IN THE BLANK:
Follow suggestions given for this exercise on page 70.
Answers:
1) to
2) him, inn
3) of
4) see
5) on

## VOCABULARY SUMMARY:

| Verbs | Nouns |
|---|---|
| are walking | road |
| see | man |
| feel | oil |
| go | wine |
| pour | wounds |
| pat | cloth |
| wrap | inn |
| carry | room |
| lay | bed |
| pay | owner |
| say | |
| will return | |

**Other vocabulary:** you, down, injured, sorry, on, his, gently, with, them, clean, tomorrow

## SENTENCE FORMATION:

Explain the example. Give other examples, if necessary. When appropriate, explain tense and person changes that occur in this exercise.

## READING:

1) True/False: 1-T, 2-F, 3-T, 4-F, 5-T.

2) Discussion section: The question raised is the wrong one; the issue is not "Who is my neighbor?" Rather, the passage concerns being a neighbor to all men.

   a) Read together 1 John 3:18: "My children, we should love people not only with words and talk, but by our actions and true caring."

   b) Question for students: What is a neighbor?

   c) Additional verses: Matthew 5:16; Titus 3:5–8; Ephesians 2:8–10.

Sequence #14: Jesus Is Crucified (Luke 23:26, 33)

**REVIEW WITH STUDENTS:** Choose some of the following items for review before beginning this sequence: vocabulary, questions, alphabet, numbers, colors, survival texts (optional), previous sequences, expansion activities.

**TAKE NOTE:** Do this sequence with a reverent spirit. Note that "keep" is often used with verbs for the present continuous tense (keep walking, keep talking).

## *TEACHING THE SEQUENCE STEP BY STEP*

### A. SET UP THE PROPS (1–2 minutes)

### B. TPR NEW VOCABULARY (10–15 minutes)
**Verbs:** watch, rest, get (up), keep, crucify, pray
**Vocabulary:** over, crowd, by, soldier, cross, back, tired

### C. MODEL (5 minutes)
1) Everyone is observing you.
2) Read and act out the Bible Sequence several times.

### D. TOGETHER (5 minutes)
1) "Now you are going to do this with me."

### E. HESITATE (5 minutes)
1) Say each line, but you hesitate before performing.

### F. JUMBLE (5 minutes)
1) Give commands from the text in random order.

### G. READING AND WRITING (15 minutes)
1) Students now open their books to the sequence pictures.
2) Read Sequence #14 to them. They follow the pictures.
3) Students write the sequence lines below each picture.
4) Read the sequence two or three times. Students follow the written words.
5) TPR the pictures.
6) Pause for questions and to point out language subtleties.

### H. SPEAKING (10 minutes)
1) Do **Backward Build-up** for each line of the sequence.
2) Repeat the Bible Sequence in normal speech. Speak slowly.
3) Listen for major pronunciation problems.

### I. ROLE REVERSAL (10 minutes)
1) One or more students direct you through the sequence.
2) Assign sequence lines to students.
3) One student directs another.

### J. SMALL-GROUP WORK (15–20 minutes)
1) Students direct each other. Books are closed, except for the speaker's.
2) Combine these techniques: **Hesitate, Jumble** and TPR the pictures.
3) Circulate around the room to encourage and help.

## EXPANSION ACTIVITIES: (Refer to Chapter 5.)

Are students ready for more Expansion Activities? (Refer to pages 80–84.)

## PRONUNCIATION:

Follow the suggestions given in Chapter 8. Focus on the sounds, not on teaching the vocabulary in this section.

## WORD ORDER:

Follow suggestions given for this exercise on page 70.
Answers:
1) Walk over to the crowd.
2) Watch Jesus go by.
3) Put the cross on your back.
4) You are tired.
5) Keep walking.

## FILL IN THE BLANK:

Follow suggestions given for this exercise on page 70.
Answers:
1) on
2) Carry
3) are
4) are
5) your

## VOCABULARY SUMMARY:

| Verbs | Nouns |
|-------|-------|
| are coming | fields |
| keep walking | crowd |
| watch | Jesus |
| says | soldier |
| carry | cross |
| put | back |
| rest | knee |
| get up | ground |
| lay | men |
| crucify | |
| pray | |

**Other vocabulary:** you, in, over, to, by, his, behind, tired, one, on, your

## SENTENCE FORMATION:

Explain the example. Give other examples, if necessary. When appropriate, explain tense and person changes that occur in this exercise.

## READING:

1) True/False: 1-T, 2-T, 3-F, 4-F, 5-T.

2) Discussion section: Help students clearly understand eternal life in Christ.

   a) Read together John 3:16: "For God loved the world so much that he gave his only Son. God gave his Son so that whoever believes in him may not be lost, but have eternal life."

   b) Question for students: What is eternal life?

   c) Additional verses: John 5:24; John 17:3; 1 John 1:1–3; 1 John 5:11–13.

Sequence #15: The Empty Tomb (John 20:1–9)

**REVIEW WITH STUDENTS:** Choose some of the following items for review before beginning this sequence: vocabulary, questions, alphabet, numbers, colors, survival texts (optional), previous sequences, expansion activities.

**TAKE NOTE:** Do this sequence with a spirit of expectation and joy. Note the use of "un-" to reverse an action (fold, unfold).

1. You're running quickly to the tomb of Jesus.
2. Stop at the entrance to the tomb.
3. Don't go inside yet.
4. First, bend down and look inside.
5. Now, go inside.
6. Look at the strips of cloth.
7. The body is gone!
8. Pick up the head band.
9. Unfold it.
10. Fold it back.
11. Hold it against your heart.
12. He is risen

## TEACHING THE SEQUENCE STEP BY STEP

### A. SET UP THE PROPS (1–2 minutes)

### B. TPR NEW VOCABULARY (10–15 minutes)
**Verbs:** is gone, fold, unfold, is risen
**Vocabulary:** tomb, entrance, yet, first, strips, body, headband, against, heart

### C. MODEL (5 minutes)
1) Everyone is observing you.
2) Read and act out the Bible Sequence several times.

### D. TOGETHER (5 minutes)
1) "Now you are going to do this with me."

### E. HESITATE (5 minutes)
1) Say each line, but you hesitate before performing.

### F. JUMBLE (5 minutes)
1) Give commands from the text in random order.

### G. READING AND WRITING (15 minutes)
1) Students now open their books to the sequence pictures.
2) Read Sequence #15 to them. They follow the pictures.
3) Students write the sequence lines below each picture.
4) Read the sequence two or three times. Students follow the written words.
5) TPR the pictures.
6) Pause for questions and to point out language subtleties.

### H. SPEAKING (10 minutes)
1) Do **Backward Build-up** for each line of the sequence.
2) Repeat the Bible Sequence in normal speech. Speak slowly.
3) Listen for major pronunciation problems.

### I. ROLE REVERSAL (10 minutes)
1) One or more students direct you through the sequence.
2) Assign sequence lines to students.
3) One student directs another.

### J. SMALL-GROUP WORK (15–20 minutes)
1) Students direct each other. Books are closed, except for the speaker's.
2) Combine these techniques: **Hesitate, Jumble** and TPR the pictures.
3) Circulate around the room to encourage and help.

# 7

## EXPANSION ACTIVITIES: (Refer to Chapter 5.)

Are students ready for more Expansion Activities? (Refer to pages 80–84.)

## PRONUNCIATION:

Follow the suggestions given in Chapter 8. Focus on the sounds, not on teaching the vocabulary in this section.

## WORD ORDER:

Follow suggestions given for this exercise on page 70.

Answers:

1) Hold it against your heart.
2) Stop at the entrance to the tomb.
3) Bend down and look inside.
4) The body is gone.
5) Fold it back.

## FILL IN THE BLANK:

Follow suggestions given for this exercise on page 70.

Answers:

1) at, of
2) look
3) go
4) it
5) running

## VOCABULARY SUMMARY:

| Verbs | Nouns |
|---|---|
| do | tomb |
| don't | Jesus |
| are running | entrance |
| stop | strips of cloth |
| go | body |
| bend (down) | headband |
| look | heart |
| is | |
| pick | |
| unfold | |
| fold | |
| hold | |

**Other vocabulary:** quickly, of, now, against, your, you, inside, up, he

## SENTENCE FORMATION:

Explain the example. Give other examples, if necessary. When appropriate, explain tense and person changes that occur in this exercise.

## READING:

1) True/False: 1-F, 2-T, 3-F, 4-T, 5-T.

2) Discussion section: Jesus Christ is God incarnate. We must believe in Him as the resurrected Lord in order to receive eternal life. Believing is seeing.

   a) Read together John 20:25,26,28, "Thomas said, 'I will not believe it until I see the nail marks in his hands...' Jesus said to Thomas, 'Put your finger here. Look at my hands. ... Stop doubting and believe.' Thomas said to him, 'My Lord and my God!' "

   b) Question for students: Do you believe in Him?

   c) Additional verses: John 1:1,14; John 10:30; John 14:9; 1 Peter 1:8.

# Prop List

Do not let props become a hassle for you; plan ahead. Be creative and improvise when necessary. Select from the "Real" or "Toy" category and supplement these items with pictures. After each lesson, keep the new props out and continually use them as part of review.

| | **Real** | **Toy** | **Picture** (photo or drawing) |
|---|---|---|---|
| Sequence #1 | apple | apple<br>tree | tree |
| Sequence #2 | knife<br>wood<br>rope | knife<br>wood<br>rope | mountain |
| Sequence #3 | sandals<br>stick | sandals<br>stick<br>snake | bush |
| Sequence #4 | coat (armor)<br>stones (5)<br>bag<br>sling | | |
| Sequence #5 | | house | house<br>tree |
| Sequence #6 | gift (box) | doll | star |
| Sequence #7 | pitcher<br>barrel<br>grape juice<br>a glass<br>water | | wine<br>water<br>barrel |
| Sequence #8 | biscuits<br>paper<br>bag<br>baskets<br>balls of paper (pieces of food) | fish | fish<br>biscuits |

| | Real | Toy | Picture (photo or drawing) |
|---|---|---|---|
| Sequence #9 | towel<br>pan of water | | |
| Sequence #10 | seeds<br>rocks<br>weeds<br>can | | rocks<br>ground<br>weeds |
| Sequence #11 | coins<br>broom<br>rug | | furniture<br>rug |
| Sequence #12 | rock<br>flowers | treasure<br>flowers | treasure<br>tree<br>rock<br>bushes<br>flowers |
| Sequence #13 | oil<br>grape juice<br>cloth | | room<br>bed<br>inn<br>oil<br>wine |
| Sequence #14 | cross | cross | cross |
| Sequence #15 | cloth<br>headband | | tomb |

# How To Adapt The Lessons To More Advanced Students

A. **INTRODUCE THE BIBLE SEQUENCES** by using a storytelling technique. That is, expand the sequences into stories told in your own words, using the pictures as your guide. An example of this technique is at the top of page 84. Work with the entire story or in sections of three to four frames at a time. At first, students listen a few times without seeing the pictures. Then they follow the pictures as the story is retold.

1) As you retell the story, keep the vocabulary and verb tenses consistent, even if you introduce a few new words. But do not allow the story to vary *wildly* between each telling.

2) Begin to ask questions about the story as suggested in Expansion Activities "A," pages 80 and 82. Do students understand the entire story?

3) Next, have students ask you questions about your story.

4) Proceed to the Expansion Activity, "Retell A Sequence," on page 84, followed by questions from the teacher and fellow students about their story.

5) The following Expansion Activities (pages 80–84) can be used to continue working with the story: "Teacher Describes a Picture," "Students Describe Pictures," "Embellish the Story," "Listen and Summarize," "Students Invent a Variation of the Original Story," "Retell Abbreviated Stories" and "Students Write Their Own Stories."

B. **AFTER STUDENTS ARE COMFORTABLE WITH THE STORY,** do the "Discussion Section" provided in each lesson plan (#2 under the Reading section). Probe their understanding of spiritual truth. Share your thoughts. Listen to theirs.

C. **USE AN ITEM OR THEME FROM THE BIBLE STORY** as a springboard for further discussion. For example, with Sequence #7, "Wedding at Cana," spend time discussing weddings. Share about weddings you have attended. Bring in pictures. Ask about wedding customs in their homeland.

D. **AS NEEDED, DO THE PRONUNCIATION EXERCISES,** teach the "how to's" of Chapter 8 and teach specific grammatical features using TPR (page 176).

E. **DESIGN YOUR OWN TPR LESSONS** that would be of interest to your students (pages 43–44).

F. **BE AWARE** that more advanced students often need help with pronunciation, idioms, slang, spelling and vocabulary expansion, especially adjectives and adverbs.

# "In-Hand" Teacher's Notes and Language Handouts

# Quick-Reference Expansion Activities List

## A. FOR ALL STUDENTS

1) Teacher asks simple questions:  Yes/no?
   Where?
   Who?
   Is this _____?

2) Students ask similar questions.

3) Teacher starts substitution drills.

4) Teacher starts question-chain drills.

5) Students jumble and match pictures from the Bible Sequences.

6) Teacher describes pictures from the Bible Sequences.

7) Teacher makes deliberate mistakes.

8) Teacher pauses in storyline.

9) Students create their own sequences.

## B. FOR MORE ADVANCED STUDENTS

1) Teacher asks what, why, how questions.

2) Students ask similar questions.

3) Students change tenses.

4) Students describe sequence pictures.

5) Teacher starts transformation drills.

6) Teacher/students embellish the sequence storyline.

7) Students listen to the embellished version and summarize it.

8) Students retell a sequence from the pictures without text.

9) Students invent a variation of the original storyline.

10) Students retell abbreviated stories.

11) Students write their own stories.

# How to Direct the Pronunciation Exercises

## A. LISTEN AND REPEAT

First pronounce each word going down and across each column. Students listen. Then do it again with students repeating. Next contrast sounds from each column with the other sound.

1) For example, in Sequence #1:  seat/sit    cheeks/chicks    bean/bin
                                  feel/fill   heat/hit

2) Students listen first and then repeat.

## B. LISTEN AND REPEAT, SOUND 1, SOUND 2

The words here are pairs that contrast minimal differences in sounds.

1) **Students listen and repeat.**

2) **Same or different?** The teacher repeats two words and the students try to discern if the words are the same or different.

   For example:  "cheeks/cheeks"     "Are they the same or different?"

3) **Sound 1 or Sound 2?** The teacher repeats a word from one of the columns. Students determine if the word is from the Sound 1 or Sound 2 column.

   For example:  "chicks"     "Do you hear Sound 1 or Sound 2?"

4) **Which word is different?** The first, second or third? The teacher repeats the same word two times and a different word once.

   For example:  "cheeks"      "chicks"            "cheeks"

   The student listens for the word that is different.

5) **"TPR" the words.**

   For example:  "Touch cheeks."
                 "Don't touch the meat, touch the mitt."

6) **Role reversal.** As students are able, have them assume your role as the teacher in doing the exercises.

# How to "TPR" Grammatical Features

Many grammatical features can be introduced and practiced using TPR. Below are some examples. Those grammatical features that require a higher level of comprehension and verbal response should be used for more advanced students.

**A. OBJECT PRONOUNS** (me, you, him, her, it, us, them)
Teacher: "Give me the book." (Teacher **Models,** with gestures.)
Student performs the action.
Teacher: "Give the book to him."
Student performs the action.

**B. POSSESSIVE PRONOUNS** (my, your, his, her, our, their)
Teacher: "Touch your head."
Teacher: "Point to my head."
Teacher: "Hit his arm."

**C. DEMONSTRATIVES** (this, that, these, those)
Teacher: "Pick up this book and that pencil."

**D. ADJECTIVES OF COMPARISON**
Teacher: "Point to the smallest basket."
Teacher: "Give the bigger of the two books to Mary."

**E. REFLEXIVE PRONOUNS**
Teacher: "I am pouring myself a glass of water. Nancy, pour yourself a glass of water."
Teacher: "I am patting myself on the back. Robert, pat yourself on the back."

**F. OTHER/ANOTHER**
Teacher: "John, here is a pencil. Here is another pencil. Here is a book. Here is another book."
Teacher: "John, give Mark a pencil. Give Mark another pencil. Give Mark a book. Give Mark another book."

**G. POSSESSIVE CASE**
Teacher: "Bill, give Ron's book to Sally."
Teacher: "Jerry, touch Joe's pencil."

**H. COUNT/NON-COUNT NOUNS**
Teacher: "Put the pencils on the table. Pick up the crayons. Touch the books."
Teacher: "Put some sugar on the chair. Give some money to Bob. Pick up the coffee."

# Phonetic Alphabet for the Bible Sequences

## VOWELS

| | |
|---|---|
| **iy** | (tree) |
| **I** | (it) |
| **ɛ** | (bend) |
| **ey** | (taste) |
| **æ** | (bag) |
| **ʌ** | (mud) |
| **ə** | (again) |
| **a** | (hot) |
| **ɔ** | (cross) |
| **ow** | (grow) |
| **ʊ** | (look) |
| **uw** | (room) |
| **ay** | (knife) |
| **ɔy** | (coin) |
| **aw** | (down) |
| **3r** | (over) |
| **ar** | (sorry) |
| **ɔr** | (your) |

## CONSONANTS

| | |
|---|---|
| **p** | (pick) |
| **b** | (both) |
| **t** | (take) |
| **d** | (dime) |
| **k** | (cut) |
| **g** | (go) |
| **s** | (son) |
| **z** | (says) |
| **š** | (she) |
| **ž** | (treasure) |
| **č** | (chew) |
| **ǰ** | (jump) |
| **f** | (follow) |
| **v** | (very) |
| **w** | (water) |
| **y** | (you) |
| **h** | (hole) |
| **θ** | (thirsty) |
| *th* | (the) |
| **m** | (my) |
| **n** | (not) |
| **ŋ** | (sling) |
| **l** | (lay) |
| **l** | (oil) |
| **r** | (road) |

# How to Pronounce Plurals

### RULE #1
After a voiceless sound
(**p, t, k, f,** θ), the "-s" ending
is pronounced **s.**

### EXAMPLES
cats, snakes, stamps, jokes, sports,
baths, likes, hates, speaks, laughs

### RULE #2
After a voiced sound
(**b, d, g, v, th, m, n,** η,
**l, r,** and all vowels), the
"-s" ending is
pronounced **z.**

dogs, questions, parties, cars, things,
wears, loves, tells, says, does

### RULE #3
After a silibant (hissing)
sound (**s, z, zsh, sh, j, ch**), the
plural is formed by adding
"-s" or "-es" and is
pronounced **iz.**

glasses, surprises, boxes, dishes,
languages, watches, washes,
loses, hisses, changes

# How to Pronounce the Past Tense

## RULE #1

If the base verb ends in a **t** or **d,** pronounce the "-ed" as an extra syllable.

When the base verb ends in a **t** or **d,** the "-ed" ending is pronounced as **id.**

**EXAMPLES**

waited, decided, painted, shouted, pointed

## RULE #2

If the base verb does not end in **t** or **d,** do not add an extra syllable.

rained, laughed, played, filled, smelled, poured, walked

If the base verb ends in a voiced sound, the "-ed" ending is pronounced **d.**

rained, played, filled, closed, turned, smelled, poured, stirred, spilled

## RULE #3

If the base verb ends in an unvoiced sound (not letter), the "-ed" ending is pronounced **t.** The unvoiced endings in English are **p, k, f, s, sh** and **ch.**

laughed, brushed, watched, danced, walked, pick up, looked, talked, stopped, wrapped, checked, touched, scratched, erased, rinsed

# How to Spell the Past Tense

| **RULE #1** | **EXAMPLES** |
|---|---|
| If the verb ends in "e" just add "d." | dance=danced, rinse=rinsed |

| **RULE #2** | |
|---|---|
| If the verb ends in "y" after a consonant, change the "y" to "i" and add "ed." | study=studied |

| **RULE #3** | |
|---|---|
| If the verb ends in a single consonant after a stressed vowel spelled with a single letter, double the consonant and add "ed." | stop=stopped, plan=planned |

**RULE #4**

For all other verbs, add "ed."

# How to Spell the Present Continuous

| VERB | RULE | EXAMPLES | EXCEPTIONS |
|------|------|----------|------------|
| Final silent "e" | drop "e," add "ing" | write=writing<br>make=making | none |
| Final "ee" | keep "ee," add "ing" | see=seeing<br>flee=fleeing | none |
| Final consonant preceded by single vowel | double final consonant, add "ing" | get=getting<br>run=running<br>sit=sitting | Two-syllable words with stress on 1st syllable: listen=listening, enter=entering. Final "h," "w," "x," "y": fixing |
| Final "ie" | drop "ie," add "y" + "ing" | die=dying<br>lie=lying | none |
| All other verbs | add "ing" only | follow=following<br>look=looking<br>go=going<br>jump=jumping<br>stand=standing | none |

# English-Outreach Ministry

# Launching an English-Outreach Ministry

9

# Steps in Launching an English-Outreach Ministry

## A. A CHURCH-BASED MINISTRY

**Step One:** Gather prayer support.

An essential foundation for an English-outreach ministry is prayer support. Begin to pray and look for others to join you. Pray that the leadership of the church, and the congregation as a whole, would embrace the ministry as an important outreach of the church. Also ask the Lord to provide motivated volunteer teachers and to prepare the hearts of many students to trust Christ as their Savior.

**Step Two:** Gain the support of your church's leadership to recognize the ministry as an official part of its outreach.

This will help the congregation as a whole to identify with the ministry, lend its prayer support and become involved as volunteer teachers. Schedule a brief presentation to the congregation about the ministry's goals and needs.

**Step Three:** Select a layperson as director.

Normally, church staff are very busy and may not have the time to become involved in the details of launching a new ministry. One of the keys to a successful English-outreach ministry is finding a layperson who feels called of God to give leadership to the ministry.

**Step Four:** Outline the director's job description. Responsibilities include:

a) Recruit volunteer teachers. Teachers must be committed to the ministry as well as patient and loving with students. They do NOT need to be "gifted teachers." Of course, gifted teachers often do well with language-learning groups but, as mentioned earlier, they may have some difficulty adjusting to TPR if they cannot curb their desire to explain the language.

b) Train the teachers. If *English in Action* is used, this would involve reading the Teacher's Manual together and conducting practice sessions. If other materials are chosen, volunteers must be trained in how to use them.

c) Organize the program. This can be done as a team (with other teachers), with responsibilities delegated for:

   • prayer support

- advertising

- registration

- recruiting host families for students

- scheduling

- social and outreach activities (picnics, host meals, parties, banquets)

- teacher recognition

## B. A COMMUNITY-BASED MINISTRY

**Steps One to Four** are also important for community-based programs. An additional step can be considered:

**Step Five:** Network with other Christian organizations and agencies in your community.

Contact Christian ministries that are active in your community. This will help promote your program and will connect you to a pool of prayer support and potential volunteer teachers. Some may have classroom space that could be available for your use.

## C. A PERSONAL MINISTRY

Leading an English-outreach group in your living room can be a very effective ministry! Begin by praying and asking friends to pray with you about beginning a group. Advertise among friends in your neighborhood or apartment building. Encourage your friends to invite their non-English–speaking acquaintances to the group. Warning: If the class goes well, it could quickly outgrow your home!

# Pointers for Having a Ministry with Language Students

**A. TEACHING ENGLISH IS A RELATIONSHIP BUILDER,** so keep relationships a priority. Relationships, as you know, require time and energy. If you recruit students so that you, or someone else, can preach to them on the first day, I am afraid you will lose most of them.

If, on the other hand, you demonstrate a willingness to befriend and help them, I believe you will have some new friends in your life!

**B. DO NOT USE THE BIBLE CONTENT AS A "HIDDEN AGENDA"** when advertising for the course. Let people know in advance that biblical stories are the foundation for the content. At the same time, the English program is not a "come-on" to read the Bible; it works. The students will learn English!

**C. HOSPITALITY IS A KEY INGREDIENT** for ministry with non-English–speaking students. Hosting dinners and picnics can help you develop relationships with them.

**D. HOLIDAY CELEBRATIONS ARE A GREAT OPPORTUNITY** for students to share food and customs from their native countries and also come to understand better American customs.

**E. FOREIGNERS IN THE USA FREQUENTLY NEED HELP WITH PAPERWORK,** such as filling out forms and applications. Anything you can do in this area will be greatly appreciated by them.

**F. SIMILARLY, COUNSEL AND ADVICE ARE OFTEN NEEDED BY STUDENTS.** Put them in touch with people who can help them.

**G. A WORKSHOP OR BIBLE STUDY CAN BE AN EFFECTIVE OUTREACH.** Select a topic of interest and conduct the workshop or study in the students' primary language.

**H. CHRISTIAN VIDEOS ARE AN EXCELLENT SPRINGBOARD FOR COMMUNICATION.** Search out copies in the students' native language.

**I. INVITE STUDENTS TO YOUR CHURCH** and/or visit theirs.

**J. HAVE A COPY OF THE NEW CENTURY VERSION BIBLE** for each of your students. The NCV Bible is used throughout the Student Workbook, *English in Action,* and can serve well as a companion book for the course. The NCV was designed with the English-language–learning population in mind. It may be ordered by calling Word Publishers at 1-800-933-9673, Ext. 2037. Discounts are available for case orders.

# Other products available from Dawson Media

**English in Action:** Learn How to Teach English Using the Bible
Using the popular Total Physical Response (TPR) method, this Bible-based curriculum equips lay teachers—even those with no teaching experience—to have a ministry through teaching English. **Designed for beginning students**.
Teacher's Manual (208 pages)
Student Workbook (130 pages)
*By Wally Cirafesi*

**English in Action Storyteller**
**Designed for intermediate students**,
*Storyteller* helps students practice and build their English communication while listening to, speaking, reading, and writing stories. Using Bible stories that correlate to the students' lives, *Storyteller* encourages students to use English for practical and creative communication.
Student Workbook (122 pages)
Teacher's Manual (52 pages)
*By Wally Cirafesi*

**English in Action Training Workshop Video**
This 90-minute video will walk you through the beginner's material and the TPR method. You'll come away with the instruction and confidence you need to develop your own English-teaching ministry.
DVD
*By Wally Cirafesi*

**Unshackled & Growing:** Muslims and Christians on the Journey to Freedom
This three-part book is written for Muslims who are interested in knowing more about Jesus. The first part of the book addresses issues about Jesus and His gospel of grace, while the second and third parts are designed to help a new Muslim-background believer grow in Christ. (248 pages)
*By Dr. Nabeel Jabbour*

**Funding Your Ministry Whether You're Gifted or Not!:** An In-depth, Biblical Guide for Successfully Raising Personal Support
This unique book offers a biblical (and humorous) perspective on the attitudes and obstacles involved in raising personal support. Author Scott Morton takes readers through every step of fundraising—from calling for an appointment to making an appeal to ministering to your donors. Also includes a Bible study on fundraising. (219 pages)
*By Scott Morton*

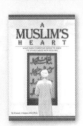

**A Muslim's Heart:** What Every Christian Needs to Know to Share Christ with Muslims
In an age when Christians are often more fearful and suspicious of Muslims than warm and relational, *A Muslim's Heart* will help you understand Muslim culture and how to share Christ within that context. A practical, quick-to-read guide, this book is ideal for those befriending Muslims overseas and in their own U.S. neighborhoods. (62 pages)
*By Dr. Edward J. Hoskins*

**Discovery: God's Answers to Our Deepest Questions**
This intensive Bible study addresses a Christian's basic questions about God and the kind of abiding relationship He wants with us. Covers such topics as, "Is God really in control?" "Does He have a purpose for my life?" and "How do I know if my faith is growing?" For new and seasoned believers, *Discovery* is ideal for small groups or individual use. (235 pages)
*By Will Wyatt*

**Here I Am: Worship Songs of the Discovery Bible Study**
Audio CD
*By Scott Lisea*

**Home Again:** Preparing International Students to Serve Christ in Their Home Countries
After receiving an international education and developing a relationship with Christ, many graduates are surprised at how hard it is to go home again. This book helps internationals and the people discipling them lay the foundation for a smoother transition home, a lifelong walk with God, and the making of disciples of all nations. (148 pages)
*By Nate Mirza*

**Meditation**
This Navigator classic has helped thousands enter into a more abiding relationship with Christ through meditation on the Word. (96 pages)
*By Jim Downing*

Post Office Box 6000 • Colorado Springs, CO 80934 • 888-547-9635 • FAX 719-594-2553 • www.dawsonmedia.com

*Dawson Media aims to help Navigator staff and laypeople create and experiment with new ministry tools for personal evangelism and discipleship.*

A MINISTRY OF THE NAVIGATORS®